POTFISHING

Secrets of Potfishing

By Edward. R. Ricciuti

ISBN 0-88839-085-8

Copyright © 1982 Edward Ricciuti

Cataloging in Publication Data.

Ricciuti, Edward
  Secrets of pot fishing
  (Northeast fishing series)

  1. Shellfish gathering. 2. Cookery
  (Shellfish). I Title II. Series.
  SH400.4.R53   799.2'55384   C81-091017-9

All rights reserved. No part of this publication may be reproduced, stored in a retrieval system or transmitted, in any form or by any means, electronic, mechanical, photocopying, recording or otherwise, without the prior written permission of Hancock House Publishers.

Editor Margaret Campbell
Typeset by Anne Whatcott in Garamond type on an AM Varityper Comp/Edit
Layout Linda Rourke
Production & Cover Design Peter Burakoff
Artwork by Barb Wood
Printed by Friesen Printers, Altona, Manitoba, Canada
Front and Back Cover Photos: David Hancock

Hancock House Publishers
256 Route 81, Killingworth, CT, U.S.A. 06417
Hancock House Publishers Ltd.
19313 Zero Avenue, Surrey, B.C., Canada V3S 5J9

Table of Contents

About Potfishing 6
Lobstering 7
Crabbing 38
Conchs 68

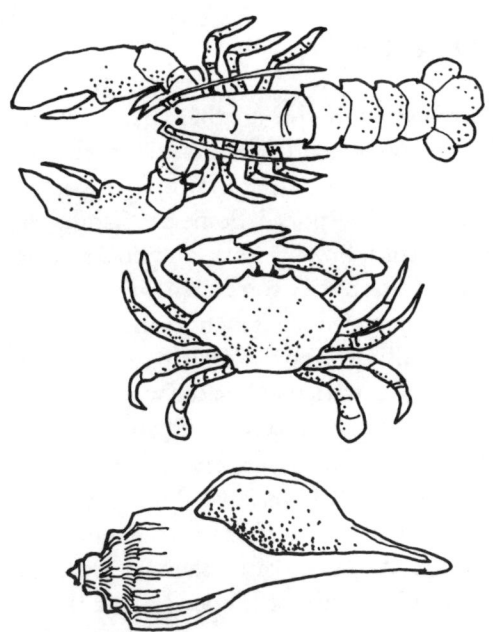

Dedication: To Good Eating

Secrets of Potfishing

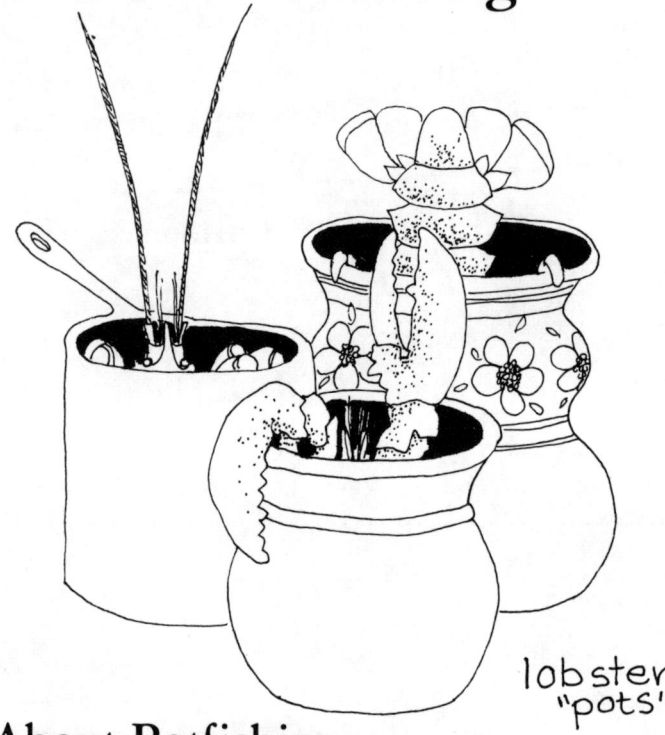

lobster "pots"

About Potfishing

The inshore waters of the northeastern United States and maritime Canada abound with lobsters and several other types of shellfish that can be easily caught in simple traps, most of which are commonly known as "pots." Some pot fishing can be carried on from shore, jetties, breakwaters, and docks. It is best done, however, from a boat. Even a rowboat or small skiff, especially if equipped with an outboard of a few horsepower, is sufficient. If you happen to be sailing or power cruising, you may want to take along a pot or two to catch a meal on the way. This book will tell you how to do it, and how to cook what you catch.

Besides lobsters, the book covers several types of crabs, and the good-tasting giant sea snails variously known as conchs, whelks or winkles. All provide the stuff of which great meals are made, and going down to the sea to catch them is great fun for those who relish the taste and feel of salt spray, and the sound of the waves.

1. LOBSTERING

...meet the LOBSTER.

Meet the Lobster

The lobster that is the subject of this book is the American species, technically known as *Homarus americanus*. It ranges from Labrador to North Carolina, although it is truly abundant only from Long Island north. South of North Carolina, the American lobster is replaced by another species, the spiny lobster. Its body has a shape similar to the American lobster, but there are some easily observable differences between the two species. The most obvious contrast is that the American lobster has large claws on its front four legs. The spiny lobster does not.

Spiny lobsters of one type or another have a wide range in the world's oceans. They live in the tropical and subtropical eastern Atlantic, from southern Europe to South Africa, as well as in the Indo-Pacific. Spiny lobsters provide the lobster tails sold frozen in food markets and served in restaurants.

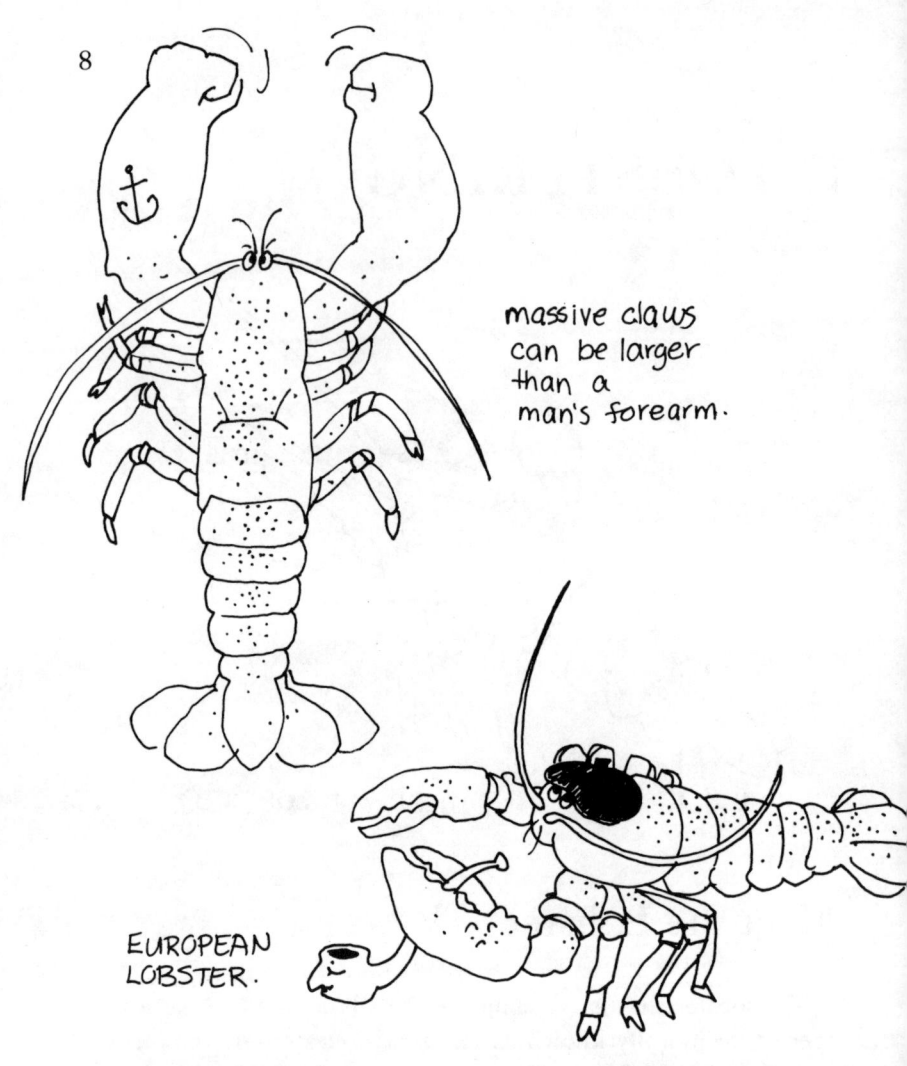

massive claws can be larger than a man's forearm.

EUROPEAN LOBSTER.

Paralleling the range of the American lobster, on the opposite side of the north Atlantic, is a closely related species. This one, the European lobster, almost exactly resembles the American type, but is smaller. Like the American lobster, the European type has large claws on its first two pair of limbs.

The first pair of claws is especially big. In fact, they can be massive, larger than a man's forearm on very old American lobsters. Anyone planning on lobstering should remember that these claws can deliver a painful wound. Stay out of their way. At the same time, keep in mind that the claws are a bounty. They contain some of the best meat in the lobster.

Lobster Lore

The lobster belongs to a vast group of animals without backbones, called arthropods. This group also includes insects, spiders, and centipedes. The arthropods range in size from animals that are virtually microscopic to giants, such as the spider crab of Japan, which has a span of a dozen feet across its spindly legs.

Lobsters and crabs are members of a clan within the arthropods called crustaceans. Other crustaceans are barnacles, shrimp, and krill, the last-mentioned a major food of many baleen whales.

Crustaceans have a segmented body, with jointed legs, and an external skeleton, called the exoskeleton, or just "shell." That much they share with other arthropods. In addition, crustaceans, large and small, have two pair of antennae.

Arthropods -
... great range in size.

Crustaceans
... segmented bodies.

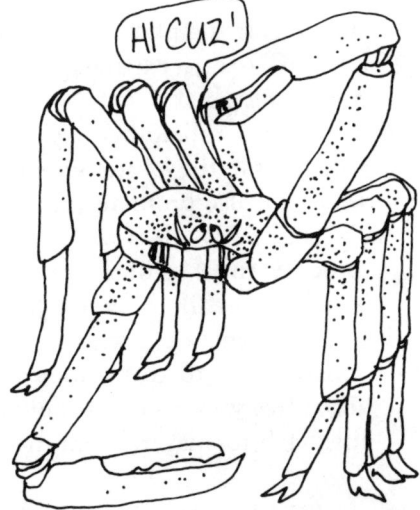

HI CUZ!

The lobster's exoskeleton is what we commonly call its shell. Unlike a true shell -- as in a clam -- the exoskeleton is periodically shed. As the lobster grows, it discards its existing exoskeleton -- we'll call it a shell to make things simple -- and develops a new one that is larger to accommodate its added bulk. Often the lobster eats its cast-off shell for its mineral content.

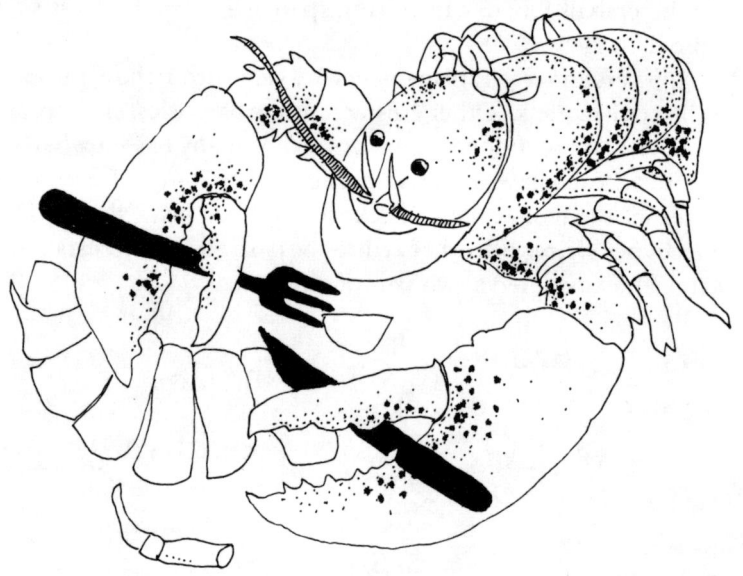

Prior to shedding, or "molting" a new shell grows beneath the lobster's old one. For a month after molting, however, the new shell is soft and pliable, and readily absorbs water. As the shell takes up water, it expands, making room for the increased size of the lobster's body.

The new shell hardens as calcium produced by special structures in the lobster's stomach enters it. Nutrients taken in with food also promote shell hardening.

Because growth is fastest in young lobsters, they molt most often. A small lobster may shed its exoskeleton several times annually, usually between June and October. By the time a lobster is about a pound in weight, the beginning of what is generally regarded as commercial size, it has reached an age of about five years and has molted about two dozen times. After this, a lobster may molt only once a year. Really big lobsters may not do so more than once every several years.

When it is time to molt, the lobster quietly lies on its side. A split appears where the body joins the tail, and from this opening the lobster crawls -- a process which can take between a few minutes and a quarter hour.

After it has molted, the lobster's temporarily soft shell makes it extremely vulnerable to enemies. One of the worst threats to a lobster at this time is another lobster. They are cannibals. Sand tiger sharks, cod, skates, and dogfish also eat lobsters, without their hard shells.

While lobsters in a tank at a fish market may seem inactive, in the sea they frequently move about, often with considerable speed. As a rule, the lobster remains on the bottom, where it walks on the tips of its legs. Its long antennae continually move, helping the lobster detect food or enemies. If needed -- say, to escape an enemy -- a lobster can swim rapidly. It travels backwards, propelled by powerfully flexing and extending its tail.

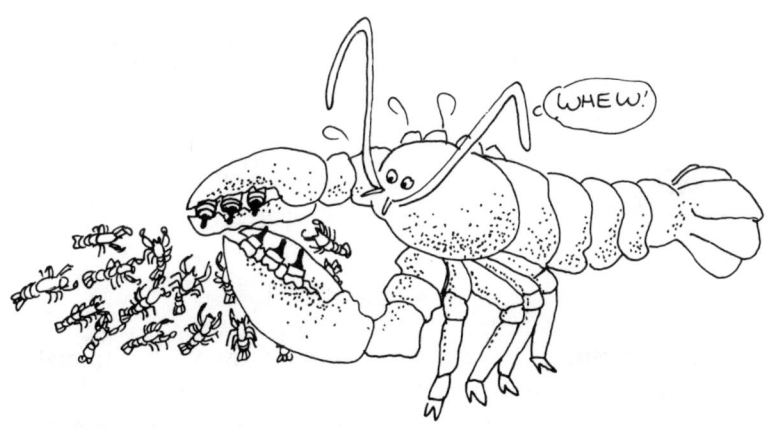

Lobsters reproduce prolifically. Generally, a lobster is about ten inches long before it spawns, although some lay eggs at only eight or nine inches long. A female of even the smallest reproductive size can carry an immense number of eggs -- about 10,000. The number increases as the lobster grows. About 75,000 eggs may be carried by a female a foot-and-a-half in length.

Lobsters mate in the warm months, just after the female molts. The male fertilizes the female while her shell is still very soft. His sperm is placed in a small pouch on her underside. When the female is ready to lay eggs she flips over on her back and forms her abdomen into a pocket. The eggs flow out of her, are fertilized as they move over the sperm in the pouch, and drop into the pocket, where they stick to appendages called swimmerets.

For almost a year, the eggs incubate, all the while stuck to the swimmerets. The female keeps her tail folded to protect the eggs, although sometimes she stretches it out and fans water over them with her swimmerets. This action keeps the eggs clean. When the youngsters finally hatch, the mother shoos them off with strong movements of her swimmerets.

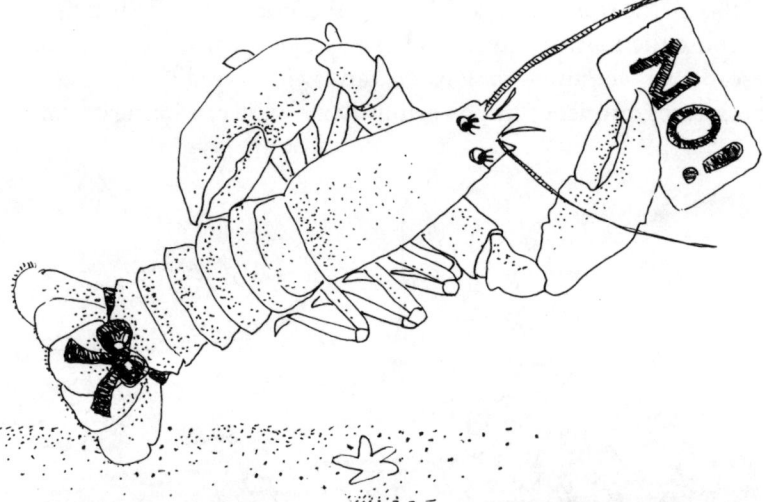

Because females can mate only after molting, younger females reproduce most frequently. Thus, although larger females lay more eggs at one time, they do so only once every few years. Increasingly, biologists suggest that for reasons of conservation the smaller females should not be taken by lobster men. Formerly, it was considered a good idea to protect the big females, but now these are thought to be a desirable catch.

Although the newly-hatched lobster can swim, it is swept here and there by the currents. At first, it remains suspended in the water, but later sinks to the bottom, where it spends the rest of its life.

Where Lobsters Live

Lobsters live from near shore all the way out to deep water at the edge of the continental shelf. Some commercial lobstermen sail up to 200 miles out in search of their catch. In colonial times, colonists could pick up lobsters in knee-deep shallows. Overfishing has ended such easy pickings, but you still can trap enough lobsters for the table in waters close enough to reach by rowboat or small skiff.

Some lobsters inhabit sand or gravel bottoms. Most favor rocks. When the tide comes up over large rock formations near the shore, lobsters often follow it. They can abound in rockpiles that are permanently submerged. Artificial rock structures, such as jetties and breakwaters, are just as good as natural ones as far as lobsters are concerned.

If you are unfamiliar with the bottom where you intend to lobster, you can pinpoint good lobstering areas with the aid of a government nautical chart. Such charts are used for navigation by boaters, and are published by the United States Department of Commerce, National Oceanic and Atmospheric Administration. They are readily available at marinas and many fishing tackle shops.

During the day, lobsters spend most of the time in burrows in the bottom, or in rocky crevices. They emerge to look for food at night, which thus is the best time to catch them.

Lobster Season

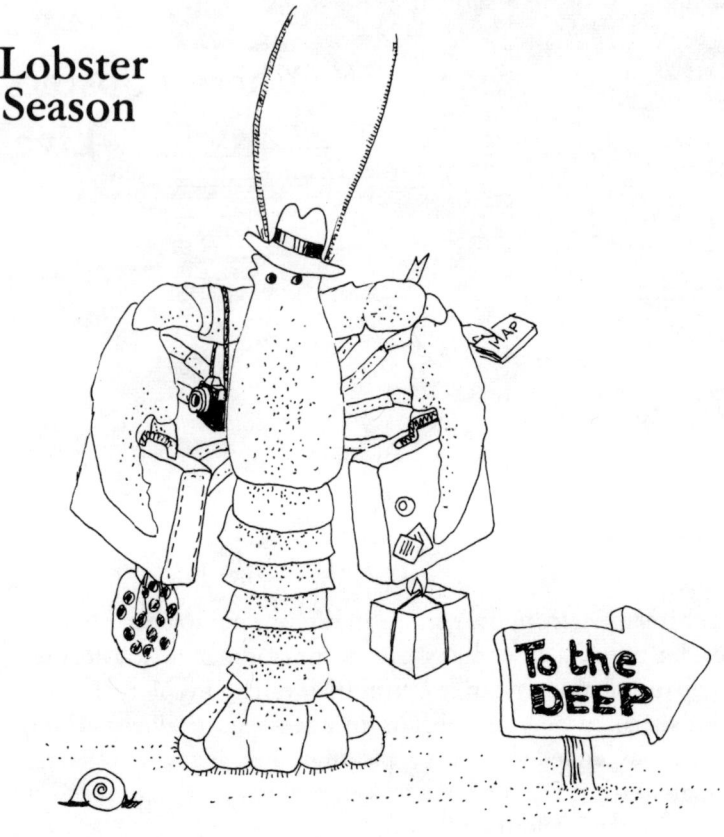

Although lobsters can be fished from inshore waters at any time of year, winter is generally unproductive for the shallow-water lobsterman. Lobsters move offshore in large numbers when cold weather sets in. Besides, fishing in winter season can be dangerous for someone without long experience and a really seaworthy vessel. Lobstering in cold weather is best left to the commercial fisherman. Once April and May roll around, however, lobsters move back to shallow water. The water is not as hazardous for the fisherman. Spring is the time to begin lobstering for the year. November is when to quit. Before you start, however, make sure you check your state's laws governing the lobster season.

Lobster Bait

People used to think of lobsters as scavengers of dead animals. True, the lobster eats the remains of its fellow undersea creatures, as well as seaweed, and sea grasses. But lobsters also are active hunters. They dig up clams and other shellfish, and eat tiny shrimp that live near the bottom. Most of all, lobsters like fish. Hidden in a hole or mass of seaweed, the lobster waits to ambush fish that swim near. Once a fish is in range, the lobster rushes out, grabs it in large claws, and feeds.

The varied diet of the lobster means that you have a wide choice of bait for it. Overall, however, fish is best. What kind of fish? Almost any will do, but why waste edible fish as bait. Fish heads are fine. So are trimmings, such as the frame of a fish that has been filleted. If you catch a fish that happens to spoil, don't throw it away, use it to lure lobsters. Spoiled fish is good lobster bait unless so soft it falls apart in the pot.

Of all fish, the best for bait are those with oily flesh. Tautog, also called blackfish, is good. So is cunner. Menhaden, or mossbunker, is excellent. Menhaden swim in vast schools, arriving in lobster waters during early summer. As they pass near the shore and into the mouths of rivers, they can be netted or snagged with a triple-pointed -- treble -- hook at the end of a line tossed from a spinning rod. They are fun to catch, too. If you can find alewives -- fish related to herring which swim upstream in spring -- catch them the same way. You can also cast for alewives with small, bright spoons. If alewives encounter an obstruction such as a dam while heading upstream they mass below it. This is a good place to net them. But check state law before you try.

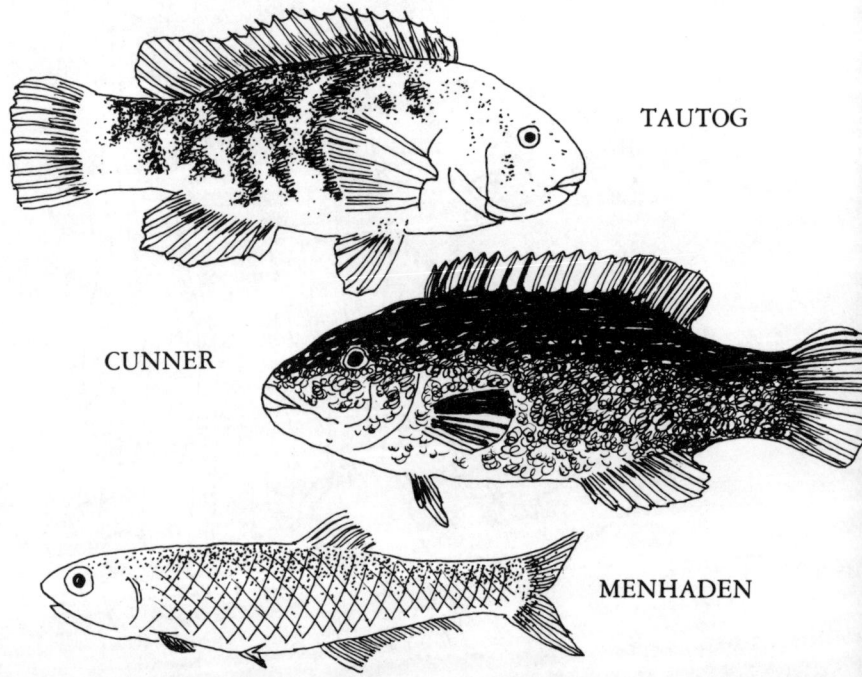

Some other lobster baits include:

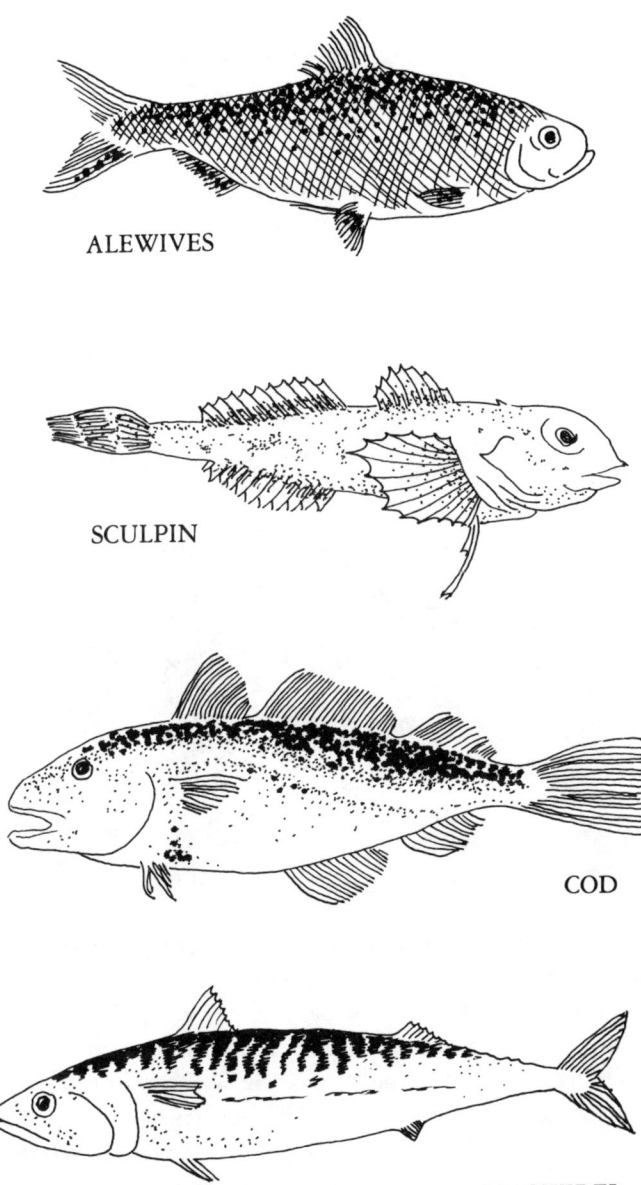

ALEWIVES

SCULPIN

COD

MACKEREL

Names of the Game

Lobstermen have some special words for their gear. Lobster traps, as noted earlier, are called "pots." Sometimes pots are fished alone, but often from "trawls." These are groups of from two to more than fifty pots tied to a heavy line in a string. This catches plenty of lobster but is not a technique for beginners. You can trap plenty of lobster for the table with just a few pots, even one if you have only a couple of people to feed.

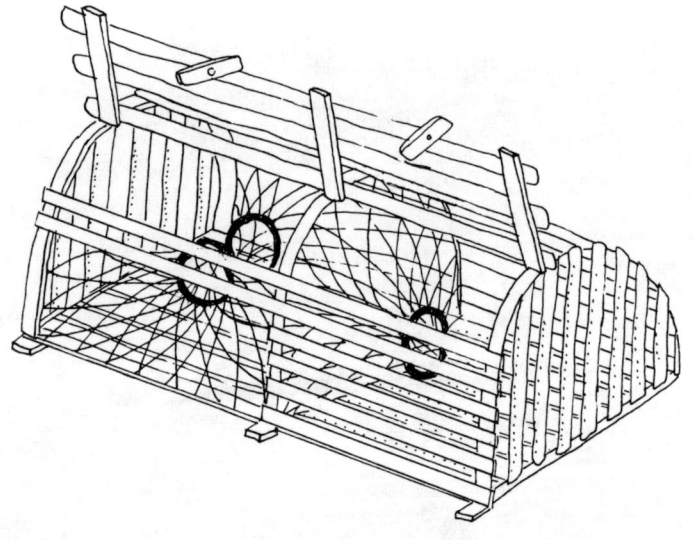

Most pots have two funnels, called "heads," through which the lobster enters. The first head leads to a compartment called the "kitchen," which holds the bait. Another head leads to a second compartment, known as the "parlor." Because of the placement and shape of the funnels, once the lobster finishes the bait it usually goes into the parlor. The pot has no clear exit from the parlor, except the small opening of the funnel, which the lobster usually cannot negotiate. Some pots have two parlors separated by a kitchen compartment.

Making Pots

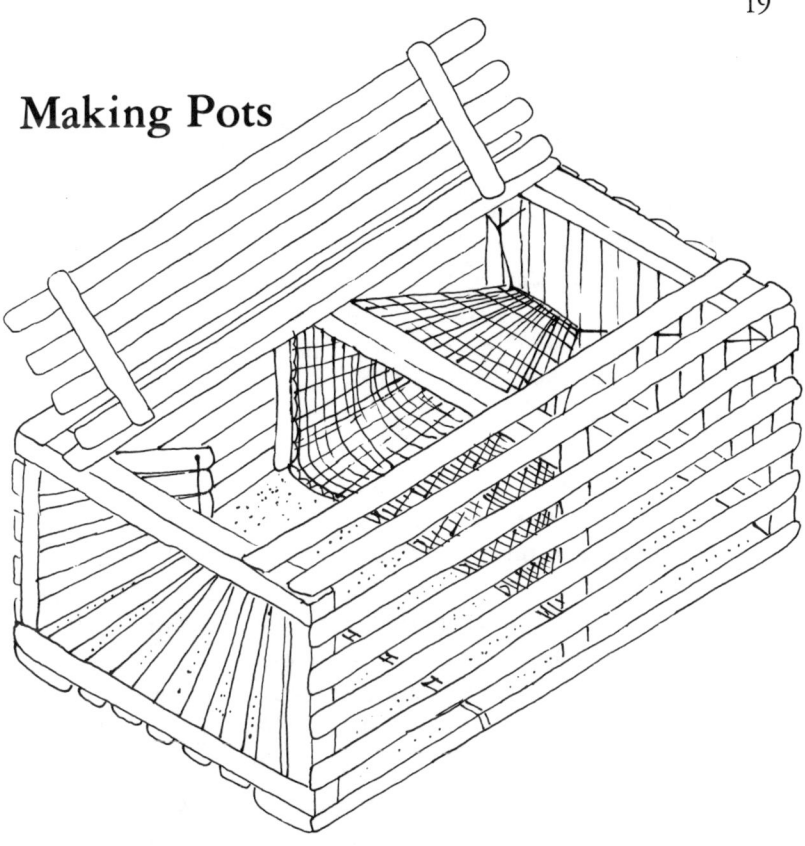

The first New England lobstermen did not have lobster pots. Instead, they used a device called a hoop-net, really little more than a bag of webbing hung from a wire hoop. The lobsterman had to stay with his net, wait for a lobster to enter it, and then quickly haul it up. Naturally, this took a tremendous amount of time, and meant that a man could fish only one trap at a time.

Modern lobster pots can be left without continual tending. These pots can be bought from many seaside shops. They are very expensive, however, and some are not really built for heavy use, but for home decoration -- like a base for a coffee table. Even if you do not plan to build your own pot, it is a good idea to understand their construction. At least this will help you purchase well-made equipment.

For the handyman, however, making a pot can be fun. Easiest of the pot designs to build is the type called a "square." It is rugged, yet light, so is very easy to use, too. Having a pot that is lightweight becomes very important when you are hauling it out of the water.

Square pots, like the one pictured here, are made in several sizes, usually from thirty inches to forty inches long. The United States National Marine Fisheries Service suggests that a pot thirty-two inches long is a good size. To make this pot, which is twenty inches wide and nine-and-a-half inches high, you will need the following materials.

Materials

-- twenty-one laths, an inch-an-a-half by three-eighths-of-an-inch by thirty-two inches
-- two runners, three-and-a-half by five-eighths by thirty-two inches
-- framing (NOTE: a recognized name for a kind of wood), six pieces, one-and-a-quarter by one by nine-and-a-half inches
-- framing, six pieces, one-and-a-quarter by one by twenty inches
-- seventeen cleat-size laths, one-and-a-half by three-eighths by eleven-and-a-half inches
-- galvanized nails, 3d, 6d, 8d sizes
-- a piece of tire rubber
-- a piece of elastic or inner tube.

Construction

First, use the 8d nails to assemble the three frames for each end of the pot and the divider (center) as pictured. It is a good idea to drill holes for the nails in the twenty-inch pieces first, to avoid splitting. Leave a quarter inch overhang.

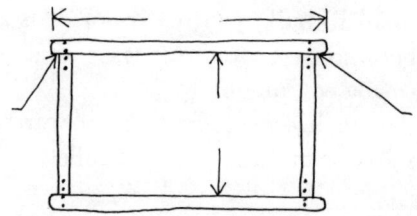

Next, attach cleats to the frames, with 3d nails. Use a half-dozen nails per cleat. The outside edges and ends of the cleats must be flush, and at least one-and-a-quarter inches apart. The spacing is to allow the escape of lobsters under the legal size. Some states have laws requiring such escape vents. Check your conservation or fisheries department before building pots.

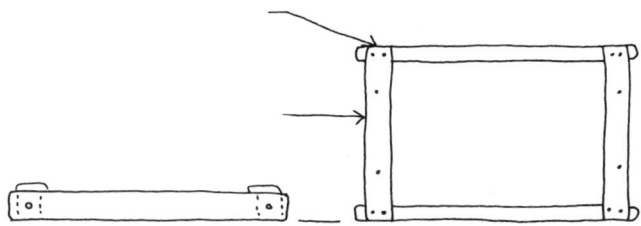

Take another frame to be the center divider. Drive four 8d nails an inch deep into the one long piece (for the cement support described later). Drive an 8d nail into each short side piece an inch from the bottom. These will be used to hold the bait band, again described later.

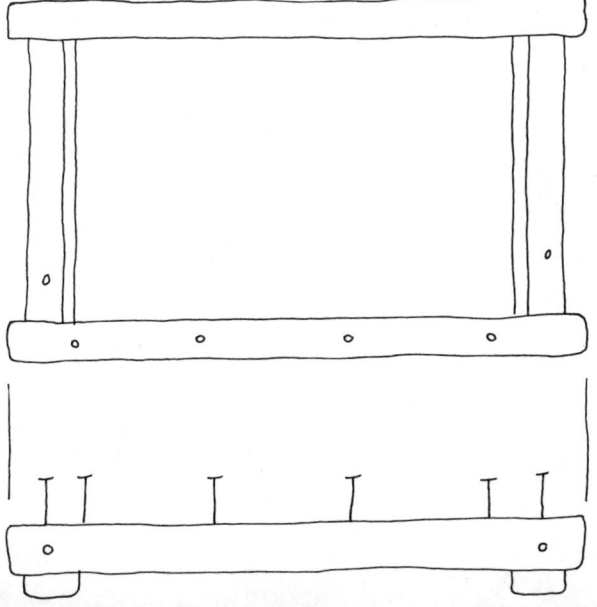

Nail the three frames to the runners with 6d nails. Place out five laths evenly (no more than one-and-a-quarter inches apart) and attach with 3d nails.

Six inches in front of the center frame, drive two 8d nails through the runners so the points project into what will be used for the cement support.

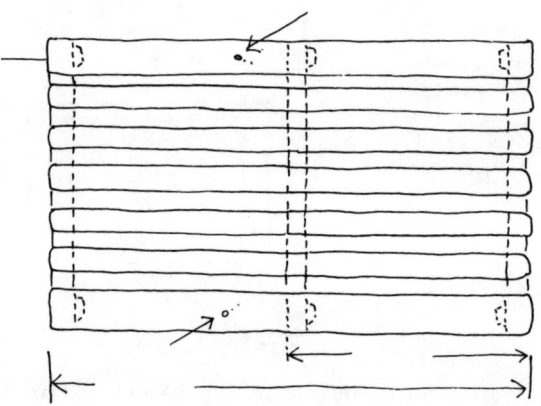

Now begin the top of the pot. As illustrated, nail two laths on each side, leaving an opening of eleven inches between the pairs for a door. Next nail four laths, evenly spaced, to each side, and under the bent cement support nails place a folded sheet of newspaper that extends an inch up each side of the pot.

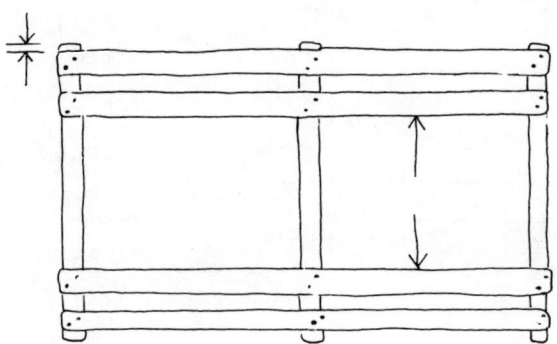

After mixing a gallon of cement, pour it over the newspaper to a depth of one-and-a-quarter inches, to a point eight inches from the center frame, toward the front of the pot. It is a good idea to place your initials or some other identification in the cement before it dries.

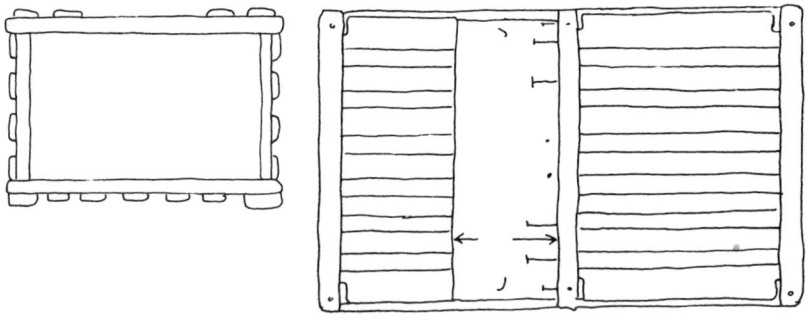

Wait until the cement hardens for a least three days before working on the pot structure again. Then begin the head, or funnel. Cut or whittle pieces of lath to form a funnel that is eight inches deep, as pictured. Drill a hole through the end of each piece. Nail them to the inner surface of the frame and shape them into a funnel form by running a wire through the holes. Tie a half-hitch in the wire after each hole is threaded. The top piece on each side of the funnel should parallel the laths on the top of the pot. The space between funnel and top laths should be no more than an inch-and-a-half.

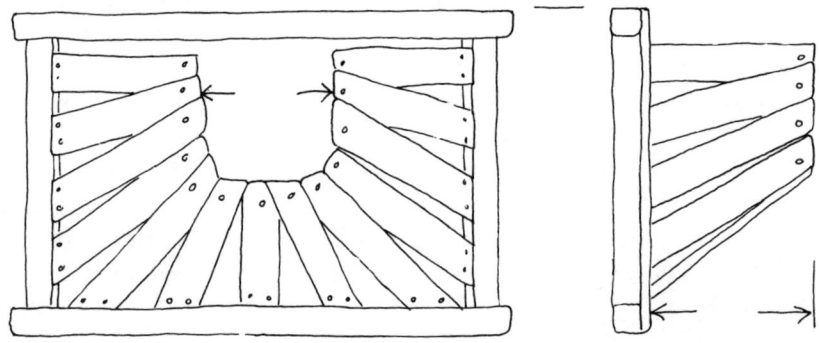

It is now time to knit the funnel from the kitchen to the parlor. Use 3/32nd-of-an-inch nylon twine. Before knitting, build another frame similar to those already on the pot. As shown, insert small screw-eye hooks on the frame's edge. Space them evenly.

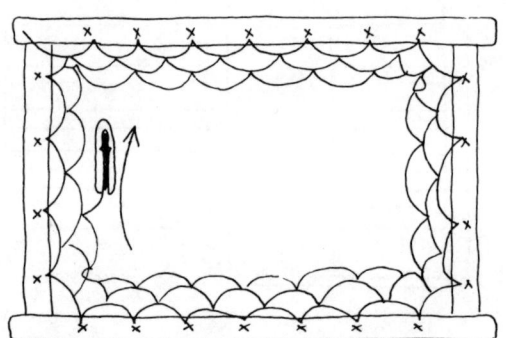
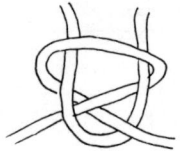

Use a standard knitting bobbin. Fill it with the twine. Steadying the frame between your knees, put clove hitches on each hook beginning at A, and leaving a two-inch piece of twine before the first hitch. The line should be slack enough that it drops about a half-inch between hooks. After finishing this step, tie a standard knitting knot in the middle of the two-inch piece of twine that was left hanging before the first hitch (as shown, before A). Then continue placing the knots between the hooks. Make a complete knitting round all the way through the hooks, creating a mesh with inch-and-a-quarter openings. At point VA take in the corner two meshes as one and continue this procedure at each corner. Continue to make full rounds.

Note: Omit taking in the corners on the fourth round. On the fifth round, take in at corners KL and RS. This is the last time to take in the corners. Keep making rounds until there are ten knots in a line going from G toward you to the left, and stop at hook G.

On the inside edge of the center frame of the pot, place 3d nails in positions corresponding to those of the hooks on the frame in which the funnel netting has been knitted. Take the funnel netting off the hooks and place it on the nails which you have just inserted in the center frame. Next bend the nails to hold the netting.

The netting must now be tied in place. From each upper rear corner of the pot run twine to the corresponding side of the funnel at the small opening. The bottom of the opening should be tight but it should be possible to raise the top enough to permit a gap of about four inches. A small lead fishing weight --about a half ounce -- should be tied to the top of the opening to keep it closed.

Now, seal off the back of the pot with cleats, attached vertically and evenly spaced. After this has been accomplished, the door should be constructed. It is made of four full laths and two cleat-size laths. Pieces of tire rubber, as shown, act as hinges.

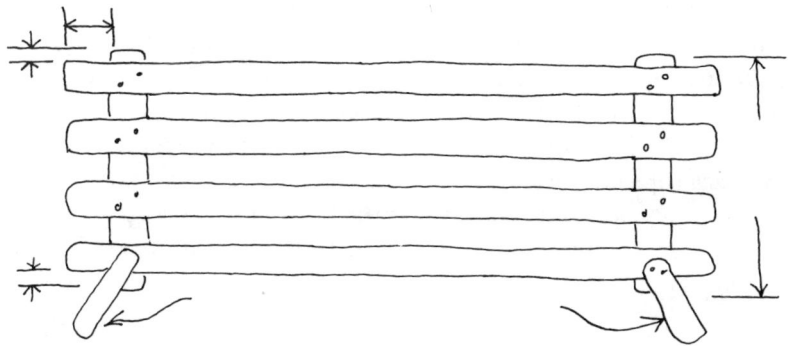

The bait band, placed on the two 8d nails in the lower front of the center frame, is made from a large elastic--the type used for a slingshot is the right size--or a piece cut from an inner tube (if you can find one). The hinges are nailed to the pot and a latch made of elastic rubber and a cleat, as pictured.

If you are a real conservationist, you may want to make a latch that degrades in salt water. This type of latch will need frequent checking and replacement, but it helps curb what is known at "ghost fishing."

Ghost fishing occurs when a pot is lost -- that is, detached from its buoy. A lost wooden pot will continue to catch lobsters for a long time before it deteriorates. Each time a lobster enters the pot it becomes potential bait for another one, because the creatures are cannibals. One way to prevent ghost fishing is to make a latch by using a hook that will corrode and a rubber band, as shown. The door described above is light enough so that when unlatched, it will enable lobsters to escape.

Lines and Buoys

The lobster pot is lowered and pulled by a stout line, which is attached to a floating marker, a buoy, when the pot is submerged. Synthetic rope, such as nylon, is appropriate for line. The diameter should be about a quarter inch. Make sure that the line is twenty percent longer than the depth of the water at high tide (check this on your marine map), so that it will stay sufficiently slack to keep from snapping as the water rises. Tie the rope as shown to both ends of the pot. A subsurface buoy of cork, plastic foam, or similarly light material can be made into a slider to keep the slack rope off the bottom (see illustration). A large knot tied in the rope about a dozen feet off the bottom will prevent the slider from climbing the line and surfacing (see illustration). When you pull the pot, the slider will drop to the end of the line.

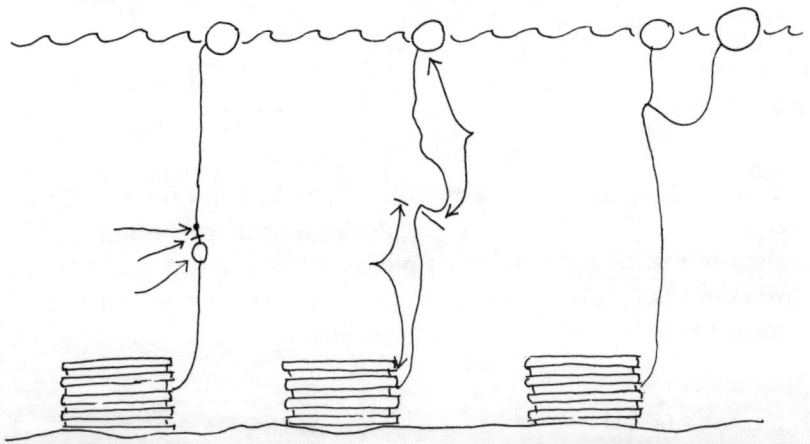

The surface buoy should be easy to spot, both for you and boaters who need to steer around it. Paint all your buoys in the same bright color. The buoy also should be readily identifiable as yours. Before painting or marking your buoys in any way, however, check your state regulations to determine whether they require a certain style of identification. Some states require that the lobsterman mark buoys with initials or social security numbers. A good way to do this is to burn in the identifying characters.

Buoys of plastic foam are sold commercially. This style of buoy has a hole through its center axis. A wood rod inserted through the hole keeps the buoy on the rod. To the end of the rod that protrudes from the water, nail a rubber strap for attaching the line (see picture). The strap, along with the washer, can be cut from an old rubber tire (**Ed. Note: not inner tube**).

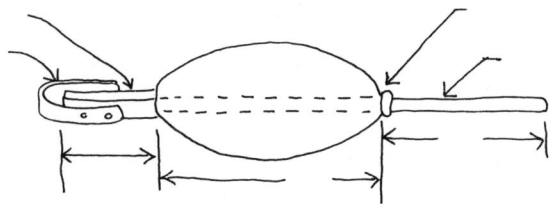

Baiting the Pot

As shown in the sketches, bait may be placed under the rubber band which you have installed on the floor of the pot. Some lobstermen set the bait on wire hooks suspended in front of the parlor funnel. Another way is to hang the bait in a small net bag (one-inch mesh). This keeps the bait from falling apart and prevents small fish from carrying it away.

The Boat

Lobstering with pots requires a boat. If you are sailing or power cruising, you have no problem. Simply take a pot or two along on your vessel. Otherwise, a small dory or rowboat suited to local sea conditions will do. In some places you can row to lobstering areas. A small outboard motor, of three or four horsepower, however, makes the process much easier. Remember that you must have enough room on your boat for pots and all other equipment.

This other equipment includes a heavy wooden crate or the lower half of a wooden barrel for holding bait and using as a platform for the pots when you are baiting or removing the catch from them. You will need some sort of tank, such as a plastic barrel or bait well, for holding the lobsters in seawater. Preferably, the tank should be equipped with an air pump, as shown. If you are only going to hold the lobsters for a short time, however, they can be kept alive in burlap soaked in salt water. The fresher and cooler (40-50° F.) the water, the better for the survival of the lobsters. They should be cooked live for the best taste.

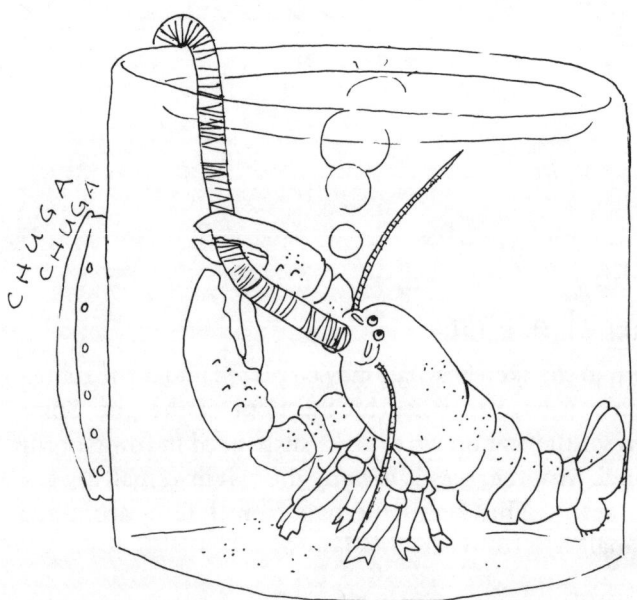

How to Fish

Under normal conditions, you can set or haul more than a dozen pots per hour. It takes only a few minutes to tend just one or two pots. Commercial lobstermen and amateurs with large strings of pots use winches to haul and set them. But you can work by hand if you have only a few pots.

Set your pots in a line about sixty feet apart, even if you are only using two. Try to locate them along a tide rip or in line with a tidal flow, but never across a channel. Hold on tight to your end of the line until you feel the pot settle securely on the bottom, or else you risk losing it if the water is unexpectedly deep. Make sure that you note the location of your pots on your navigation chart.

Try to check your pots after every night's fishing. Never leave one alone for more than two nights. Haul your pot by pulling up the rope hand over hand. Once the pot is aboard, rest it on the bait box, or between the edge of the barrel half and the rail of the boat. Remove your catch, rebait, and lower away.

Warning. Make sure all lines are neat to avoid becoming entangled. Also, if your boat has a motor, watch out that your pot line does not become snagged when you approach it. The line can snarl in the propeller or the motor.

The best approach to a lobster pot buoy is against the current and wind. A long-handled gaff can help you reach the line. While working, keep the motor in neutral.

Early morning, when the wind is lightest, is a good time to work pots. It is easier, too, on a slack tide.

Lobsters Aboard

When lobstering, it is wise to wear rubber work gloves. Besides keeping your hands warm and dry gloves guard against rope burn and the lobster's claws. Once a lobster is boated, it should be immediately checked for size. All "lobster" states have size regulations for the lobster catch, and these are strictly enforced. Gauges for determining legal size can be purchased at many fishing equipment stores. Size is measured from behind eye to the back end of the carapace, the main body shell. The tail does not count. Federal fisheries officials are conferring with

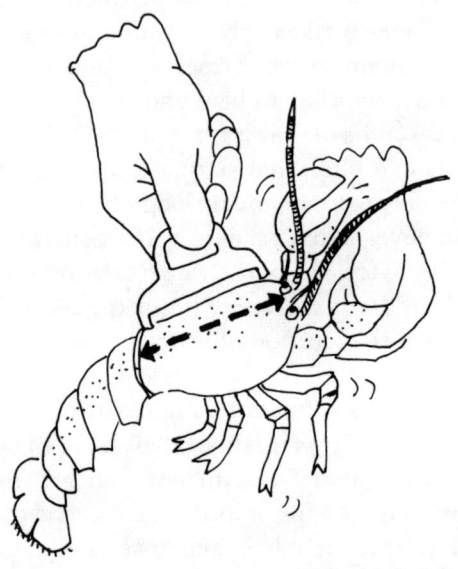

various states on how to make lobstering laws uniform. Until this is accomplished, however, there remains a bewildering variety of regulations.

Basically, however, the laws cover such things as:
-- the number of pots you can use
-- the season and fishing hours
-- markings on buoys and pots
-- types of buoys
-- size and sex of legal lobsters
-- license flags or other markers on boats
-- licensing, including boat registration
-- trawls
-- fooling with someone else's gear (dangerous to attempt, too)
-- escape vents.

the long claw of the Law.

One regulation is standard in all states. You may not land a female lobster with eggs, a so-called "berried" female. Return such lobsters to the water.

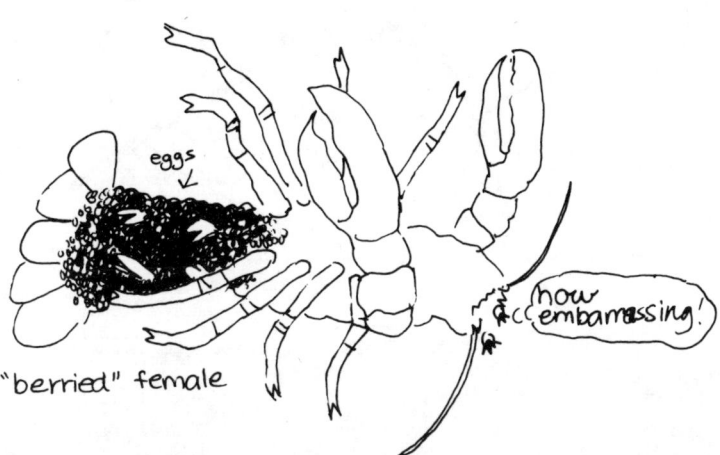

"berried" female

how embarrassing!

If you catch a lobster with a soft shell, return it to the water. Such lobsters have watery, unpalatable flesh because their tissues are filled with fluids.

To remove a lobster from the pot, hold the creature firmly on the carapace, well behind the claws. Be careful. If not, you may be pinched. You can prevent the lobster from using its claws on you, and on other lobsters in live storage, by putting a stout rubber band around each large claw. Or else you may "plug" the lobster. This technique involves inserting a small wooden or plastic peg, called a "plug," in the joint of each large claw, as shown.

Cooking Your Catch

There are many recipes for lobsters, but in New England, where lobster is king, two methods are considered supreme. One is boiling, the other steaming.

To boil a lobster, drop it alive into a big pot of rapidly boiling water, well salted and with a touch of vinegar. Leave a few inches between the top of the water and edge of the pot so it does not overflow when the lobster goes in. If you are cooking more than one lobster, put one in first, then wait for the boiling to resume, and add the next, and continue in this fashion. Boil average sized lobsters (one to two pounds) for twenty minutes.

Double the time for lobsters of four or five pounds.

Steaming time is the same as boiling. If you have a steamer, with a false perforated bottom, use it. Otherwise, a regular pot, large and with a tight lid, will do. Put two inches of salted water, with a touch of vinegar, in the bottom of the pot. Cover it. Bring the water to a boil. Drop in the lobster and let it steam. Then drain and eat.

For my money, lobster can be cooked no better way than boiled or steamed. Many people, however, relish lobster with lots of trimmings. The most famous of such dishes is Lobster Newburg, also known as Lobster House Special. The following recipe serves six.

Lobster Newburg

three live lobsters, about a-pound-and-three quarters each
1/3 cup margarine or butter
1 1/2 cups chopped fresh mushrooms
3 Tbsp. minced onion
1 1/2 Tbsp. all-purpose flour
1/4 tsp. liquid hot pepper sauce
3/4 tsp. salt
1 1/2 cups half and half (milk and cream)
3 egg yolks, beaten
3 Tbsp. brandy
2 Tbsp. chopped parsley
3 Tbsp. fresh bread crumbs
3 Tbsp. grated parmesan cheese
1/2 tsp. paprika
1 Tbsp. melted margarine or butter

Place the lobsters, head first, into a large pot of boiling water. Cover and simmer fifteen to twenty minutes until the lobsters are done. Remove the lobsters from the pot. Twist off the claws and cut off the antennae. Crack the shell with a nutcracker or hammer and remove the meat. With scissors, cut through the soft shell of the stomach. Be careful not to damage the shells. Remove the tail meat through the slit made with the scissors. Save the coral, if any. Remove and discard the stomach, setting the shells aside. Cut the meat into half-inch cubes and set aside. Melt the margarine or butter in a skillet. Add mushrooms and onions, cooking until tender. Stir in the flour, liquid hot pepper sauce, and salt. Gradually blend in the half and half. Cook, stirring constantly until the mixture thickens. Add a little hot sauce to the egg yolks. Add these to the remaining sauce, stirring constantly. Heat until thickened. Stir in the brandy, parsley, reserved lobster meat, and coral, if any. Divide the lobster mixture and scoop into the shells. Place the shells on a baking tray. Combine bread crumbs, parmesan cheese, paprika, and margarine. Sprinkle crumb mixture over the lobsters. Bake in a moderate oven at 350° F for fifteen to twenty minutes or until hot. Serve in the shells.

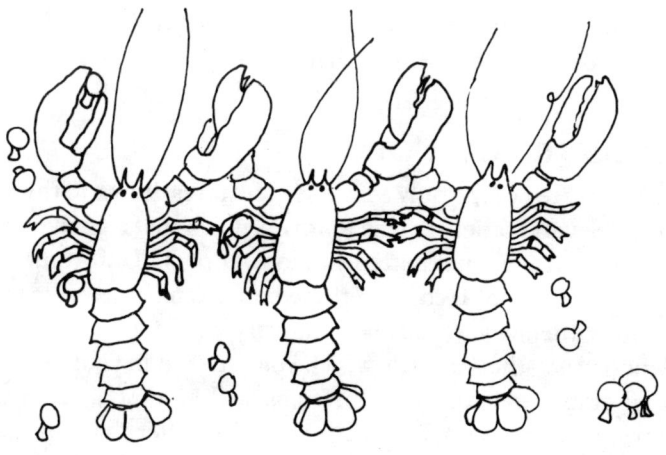

Eating Lobster

Prepare for your meal with lots of napkins, a platter for discarding shells, and a bowl of butter in which to dip the meat. First break the lobster in two, where the tail joins the carapace. You may have to twist it a bit. There is a lot of liquid in the shell. You can drink it, if you wish -- not the best table manners, perhaps, but tasty.

Crack the tail in half, lengthwise, or really any way you wish, and pull or push out the meat. Where there is a bit of black matter in the meat, remove it. This is the intestine, and it is not edible. Next, snap off the arms where they join the body. There is more liquid in the arms and claws. After removing the plugs from the claws, break them off the arms. The claws contain large pieces of meat. Crack them with a nutcracker or hammer and extract the contents.

The shell of the main body can be sliced apart on the abdomen, or even broken apart lengthwise by hand. If you see red strips in the meat, do not throw it away. The red matter is "coral," or unfertilized roe, and extremely tasty. The small legs under the body also contain meat. Break them off and either pick or suck it out.

Bonus in the Pot

Lobsters are not the only edible sea creatures drawn to the bait in pots. Several other marine animals which make good eating commonly turn up unexpectedly in lobster pots. Unfortunately, many people do not recognize these bonus catches as table fare, and throw them away, thus wasting very good food.

Among the other animals which you can trap in your pots are several crabs, and conchs. The crabs will be described in the following chapter, and the conchs in the one after that. In these chapters, you will also learn the secrets of fishing specifically for these animals.

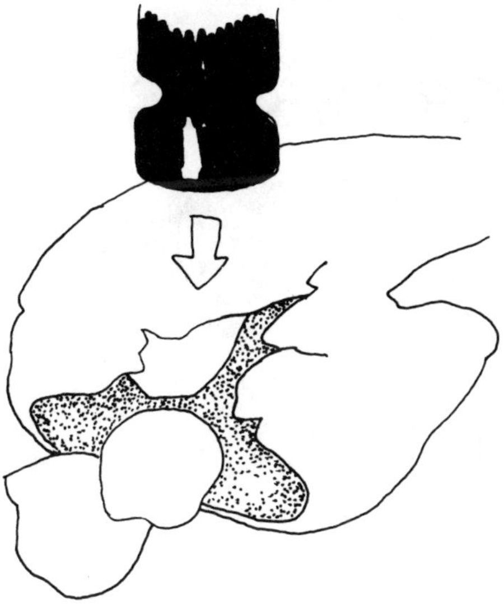

2. CRABBING

Crabs for the Table

Among the animals likely to be caught accidentally in lobster pots are spider crabs *(Libinia)*, rock crabs *(Cancer irroratus)*, lady crabs *(Ovalipes ocellatus)*, and blue crabs *(Callinectes sapidus)*. The last-named species is renowned for its tastiness, and is prime sea fare. Rock crabs are beginning to appear on the market, which is well, for they are excellent eating. Spider crabs and lady crabs seldom show up on the table, and, in fact, are considered nuisances by many lobstermen. However, they are fit for gourmets, and well worth the work it takes to prepare them.

Spider Crabs

Ugly in appearance, spider crabs often swarm into lobster pots, causing consternation among commercial fishermen because there is no market for these spindly-legged creatures. They are usually killed and tossed overboard. If you come across spider crabs in your pots, however, keep them. These crustaceans, with a leg span of about a foot, are look-alike miniature relatives of the giant Japanese spider crab, the legs of which bring high prices in markets and restaurants as "king crab." The meat in the spider crab, although admittedly not abundant, is just as delicate as that of its big cousin.

Spider crabs are brown, with shells that are covered by protuberances and a light coat of hair. They live from the intertidal zone all the way out to deep water, on virtually any sort of bottom. They are unable to swim, and travel by creeping slowly on their long but weak legs.

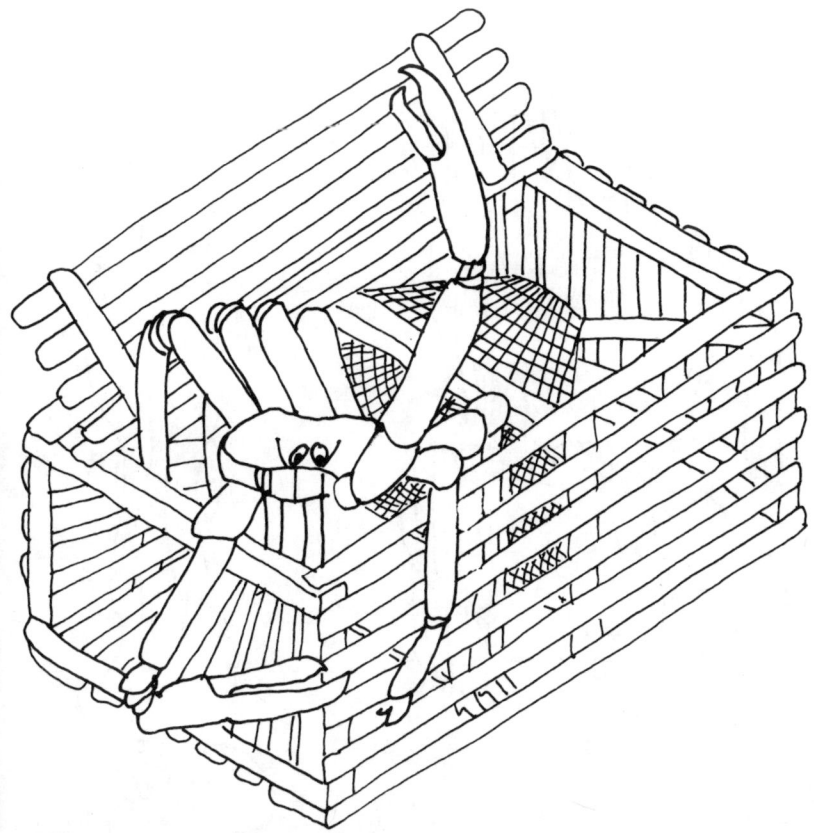

While the lack of swimming ability and slowness of the spider crab might seem to make it defenseless, it has an unusual method of avoiding predators. The hair that covers the crab entangles all sorts of algae, mosses, and even other animals such as hydroids, barnacles, and sponges. The crab, moreover, takes pains to promote the growth on its shell. It uses its small pincers to cut off bits of seaweeds, hydroids, and similar growths and plant them on its own body. The cuttings are stuck to the shell by means of a special cement which the crab produces in its mouth, and places on the material for its garden.

The contrived camouflage of the spider crab also helps it creep up on prey undetected. Spider crabs eat a variety of small invertebrates, as well as dead organic matter and plants.

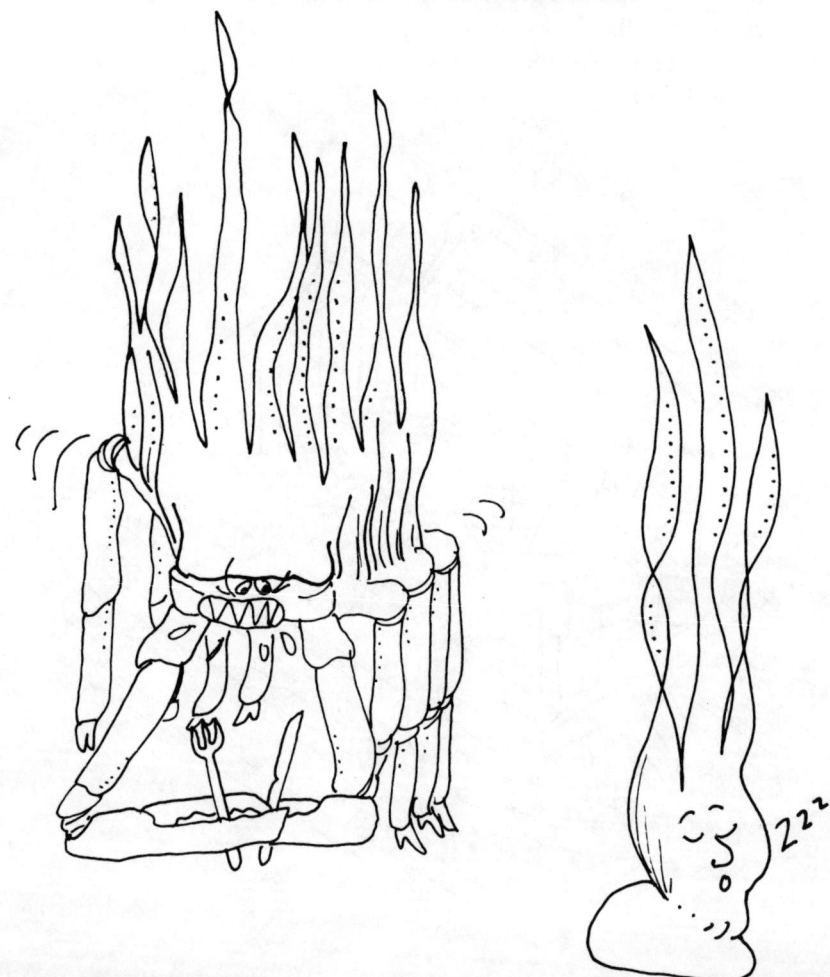

Rock Crabs

Scurrying about the shallows along the shore in New England, and in somewhat deeper water to the south, is a relative of the delectable Dungeness crab of the Pacific coast. It is the rock crab, which has a broad, oval shell, sometimes more than a half-foot wide, and yellowish, sometimes flecked with dull purple. The crab is also distinguished by heavy legs and claws. The latter can pinch like the devil, so be careful of them when handling a rock crab.

Look for rock crabs among the seaside boulders, in crevices, under stones, and in tidepools. Despite their name, they live on sand, gravel, and mud bottoms as well as in the rocks. However, they do not like water that is low in salinity, so are not found in brackish backwaters unless these are very near the open sea.

Lady Crab

During the summer months the shallows along sandy beaches are the home of lady crabs, which sometimes concentrate by the hundreds over just a few square yards of bottom. The lady crab has a shell that is about three inches wide and slightly longer than its width. The grayish-yellow background color of the shell is flecked with deep purple. This crab is an active swimmer, and hunter of minnows. Its swimming is facilitated by the flattened shape of the last pair of legs, which resemble small oars.

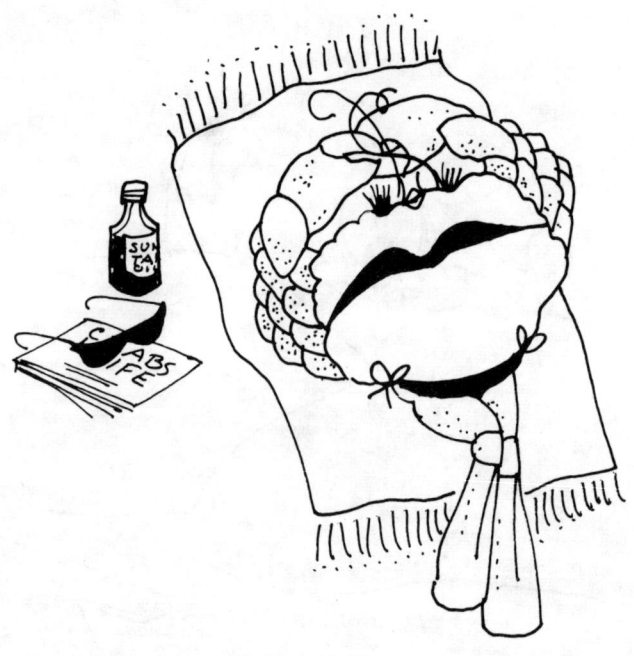

Blue Crab

Like the lady crab, the blue crab is a "swimmer" with its last pair of legs flattened into oar-like appendages. This is the best known of our table crabs, and from New Jersey south, especially in the Chesapeake, is the basis for a fishery that produces millions of dollars worth of crab meat.

The blue crab is easy to identify. Its shell is very elongated, in fact twice as long as its width. The color of the shell is a pretty olive-green with blue shadings. The blue color becomes pronounced and bright on the pincers, which in females are red tipped. Watch out for those pincers. The blue crab -- and the lady crab -- wield them with verve.

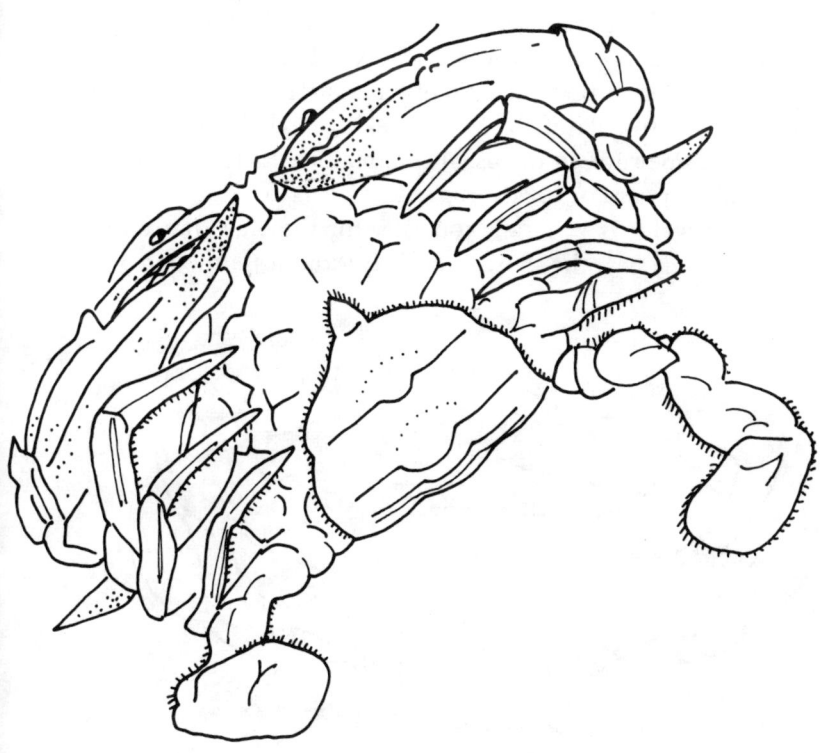

Blue crabs are found almost everywhere along the coast, except for northern New England. They are most abundant, however, south of Long Island. They seldom ever breed north of there. Pollution and hard winters have cut their numbers appreciably in New England.

The blue crab -- all crabs, in fact -- molt like a lobster. When a blue crab prepares to molt, its old shell opens along its rear edge, and the crab squirms out of it, a process which may take a couple of hours. For the first two days after molting, the crab's body is covered by a new shell that is delicate and soft. During this period, it is known as the "softshell" crab, a great delicacy. After that, the shell begins to harden, but the flesh is now thin and watery, like that of a newly-molted lobster, and just as unpalatable. The distasteful nature of the flesh is caused by the fact that since molting the crab has not caught prey and has lived on the fat in its body. By the time the shell begins to harden again, the fat is depleted, and the crab has started eating once more.

Blue crabs are omnivorous, and are both scavengers and predators. Their prey includes other crabs, including their own kind, shellfish, and finfish. While seeking food, they either swim or crawl, sideways, in the usual crab manner, although the crab can walk forward or backward.

Ocean water is generally too salty for the blue crab, so it is found mainly near the shore, especially estuaries, although in the

PINCERS:
↗ blue on boys
red on girls!

northern part of its range it migrates into deeper water for the winter. Tidal creeks are particularly favorable habitats for the crabs, so are a natural place to catch them.

The blue crab takes its adult form only after undergoing several changes in shape, occuring as the crab grows from nearly microscopic size. At one point during its growth, the young crab is likely to hitch a ride on jellyfish, seaweed, and other floating objects.

FINALLY!

By the time a crab reaches it full adult size, eight or nine inches wide, it has molted about fifteen times. The warmer it is, the faster the crab grows, and in the southern parts of their range they can mature in only six months, if they are hatched in the spring and can develop during the summer.

The female crab is ready to mate when she is about to molt for the last time. When the female attracts a male he picks her up in his crawling legs and carries her around under him as he swims. His grip is so firm he will not let go even when he and his mate are picked out of the water. The grasp is not broken until the molt is just ready to begin. Then he drops the female and stands by until she sheds, after which they mate. He remains with her as a guardian until the new shell is hard and she is armoured once more. The female then departs, carrying enough eggs to reproduce for several years.

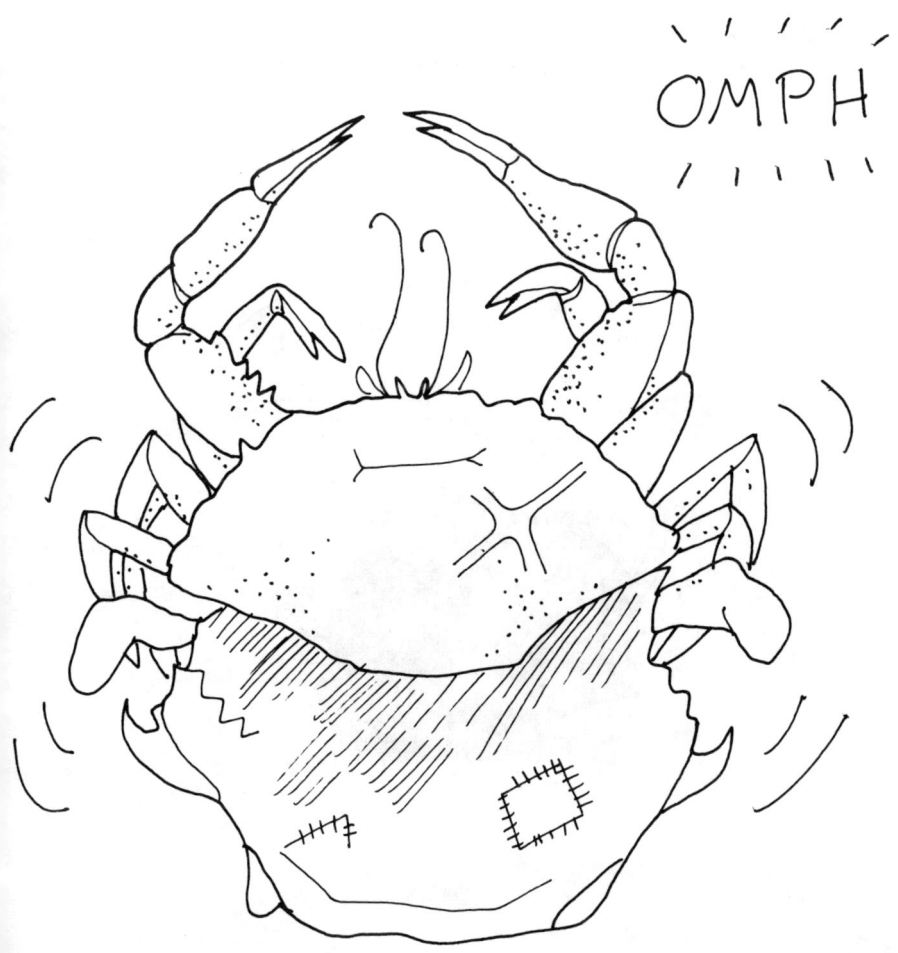

Potfishing for Crabs

There are several ways to catch crabs. Potfishing is the most efficient, getting you the most crabs for your time. No matter what method you use, there are a few considerations to think about first.

Before you start crabbing, make sure you know the laws governing the fishery. The regulations differ from place to place, and also between species of crabs. You may be risking arrest if you do not understand the rules about what kinds of crabs you can catch, how many you can keep, and the legal season.

Although the length and time of legal crab seasons vary, they always cover at least most of the spring and summer, and often extend into winter. Spring and summer are the best time of year for catching crabs, especially in northern areas, where they usually retreat into deeper water during cold weather.

Collapsible Traps

If you don't mind constantly tending a trap, there are two collapsible types which can provide good hauls of crabs in just a few hours fishing. As you can see from the illustrations, one is in the shape of a rectangular box, the other a star. I prefer the star trap, but this is strictly a personal prejudice. My only reason is that it is easiest for me to handle.

These traps collapse when they are lowered to the bottom from a boat or pier, or tossed into the water from shore. If you are tossing your trap -- a method you may have to use when crabbing on broad, shallow creeks -- make sure that it lands in the water bottom down. A chicken neck, chunk of eel, or other bait tied in the center of the trap's bottom will draw crabs, if any are around. Often, however, you will not be able to see the trap in the water, so will have to use your best "guestimate" of how long it takes to attract the crabs. The traps are constructed so that lines leading to the sides, as shown, are linked to the pull cord in your hand. When you haul the trap from the water -- do it smartly but don't yank -- the trap closes, capturing whatever crabs are inside. If you are unsure of how long to wait before pulling your trap, vary the times it is on the bottom. As a general rule, when crabbing with a trap in murky water, I let it remain on the bottom for about five minutes before my first haul. If crabs are caught, I cut bottom time in half, although I extend it again if a short wait is unsuccessful.

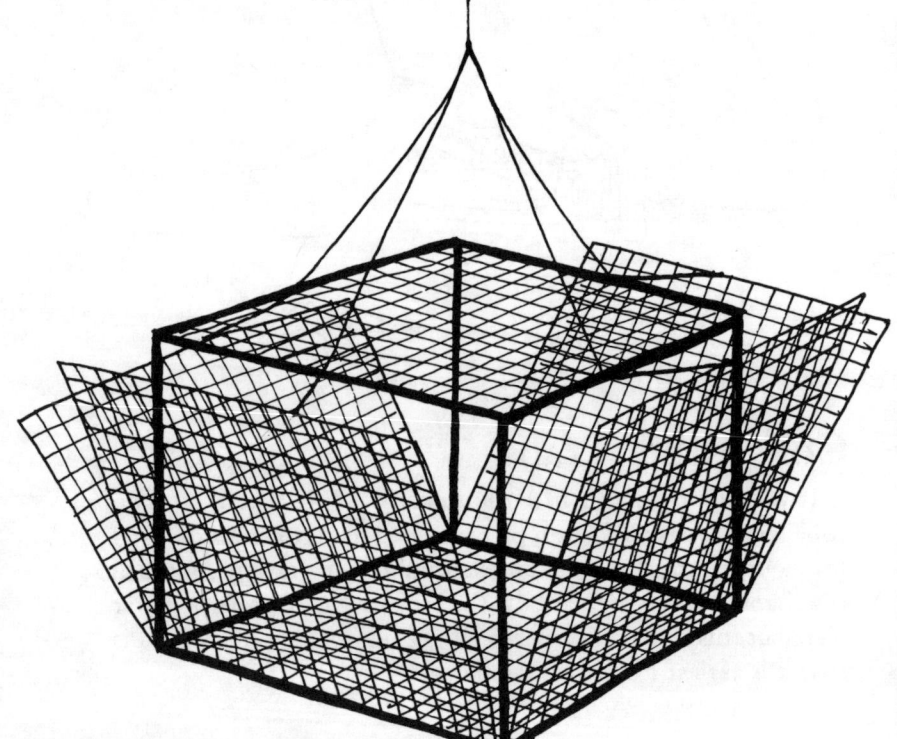

The Trotline

In terms of the numbers of crabs that can be caught, fishing with a trotline from a boat can be superior to using pots. The trotline is a length of cotton or hemp rope, up to 100 yards long, three-eights inch diameter, weighted at each end, and baited every yard. Besides the rope, you need:
-- two short lengths of chain, about a yard long each
-- two weights (use lead diving weights, cement blocks, or similar materials, weighing several pounds each -- how much depends on the currents)
-- four lengths of rope, each twenty feet long
-- strong cord -- hand-lining fishing cord is great.

The long rope is the bait line. Attach a chain to either end. To the other end of each chain, tie one of the short ropes. Each of these leads to a float -- you can use a lobster buoy or a large empty plastic bleach or detergent bottle. Use the remaining two ropes to tie the anchor weights to the floats. At intervals of a yard, tie your bait to the main rope. Use beef tripe, salted eel, bacon rind, chicken necks, or other bait that will not fall apart.

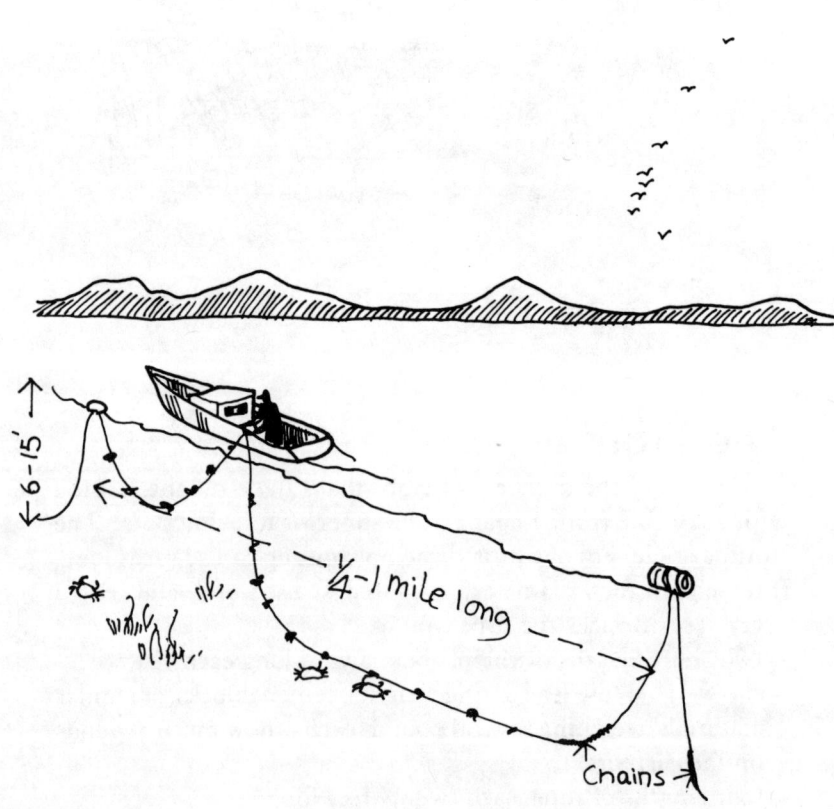

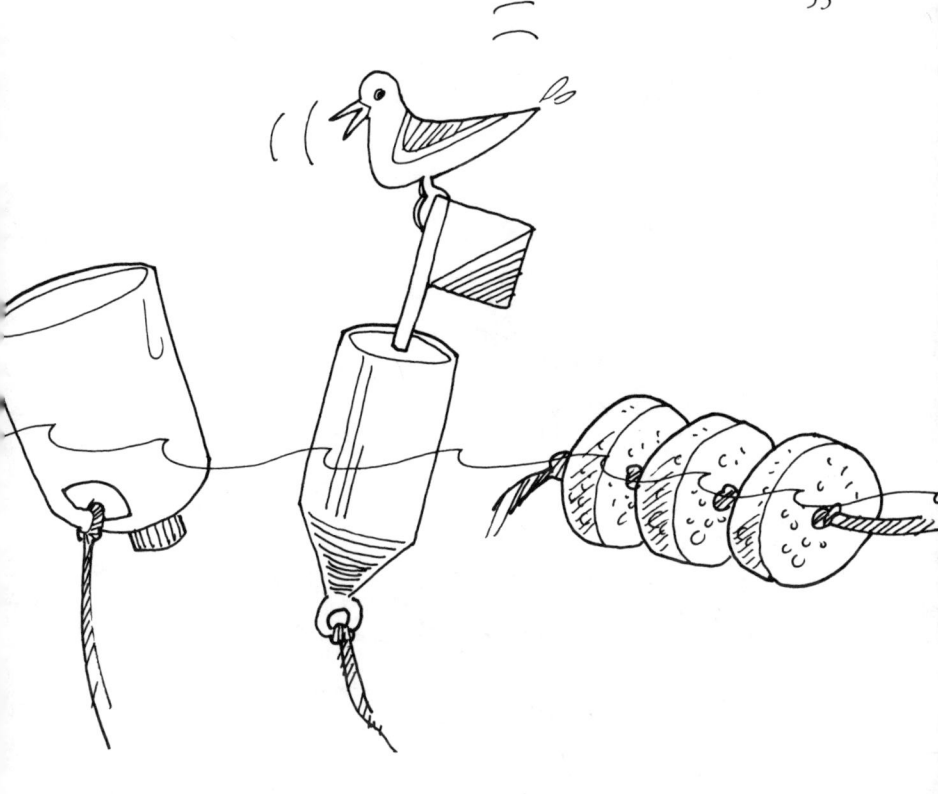

The line should be coiled and placed in a solution of brine, four pounds salt to five gallons water. This is a good way to store bait and line. Keep your line neatly coiled when you go aboard your boat. When you get to a good crabbing site -- no deeper than twenty feet at high tide -- drop the anchor weight of one end of the rope. Let your boat drift with the wind and tide and pay out the line. When you get to the end of the line, drop the second anchor. Return to the other end and get ready to crab.

If crabs are down below, they will come to the bait to feed. Slowly pull up the trotline. Go easy so you will not scare the crabs. The trick is to draw the crabs close enough to net them. If two people are aboard the boat, one can work the line while the other nets. Slowly work the net under the crab, then bring it up swiftly. Keep your crabs in a bushel or similar container (see Storing Crabs).

Crab Pots

Although not legal in all places, including some local areas as well as some entire states, crab pots are popular where allowed by law. The crab pot can be purchased at hardware and sporting goods stores in areas where it is used. Or it can be home-made, at least as easily as the lobster pot. Basically, the crab pot is a cube, each surface of which is twenty-four inches square, and made of chicken wire -- of an inch or inch-and-a-half mesh, galvanized. The pot is held rigid by a frame. Make it of metal rods welded or bolted together. You may want to go to a local welder and have him do it for you. Fasten the sides with wire, which can be undone.

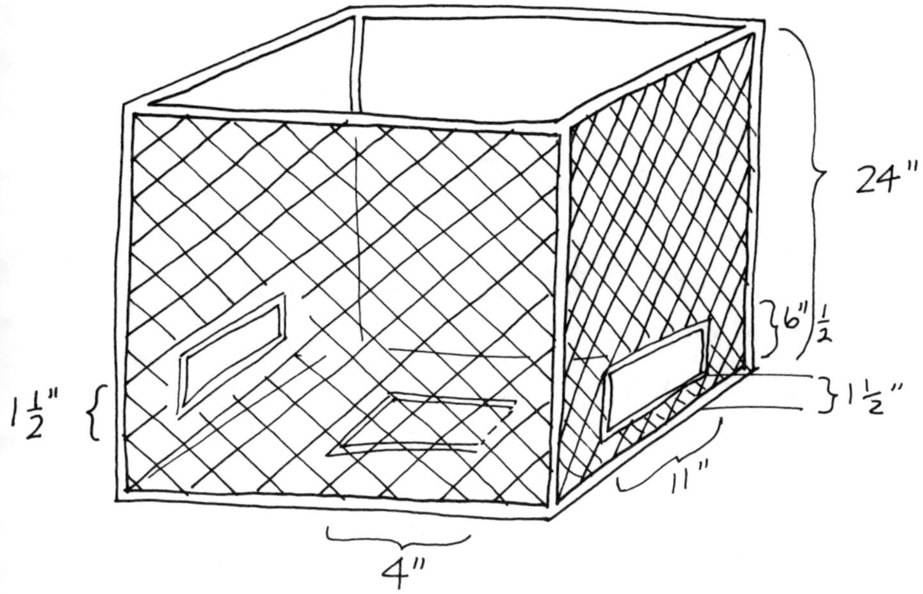

goods

The pot has two entrances, opposite one another. These are an inch-and-a-half above the floor of the trap. Cut away the chicken wire for eleven inches horizontally and six-and-a-half vertically. Inside each entrance, place a funnel five inches long made of the same poultry wire. The mouth should match the eleven by six-and-a-half-inch entrance. The opening of the funnel within the trap should be five-and-a-half by two-and-a-half inches. Next, in the center of the pot's floor make a door four inches square, but do not cut the wire on one side, leaving it as a hinge. This is the opening by which you will insert bait.

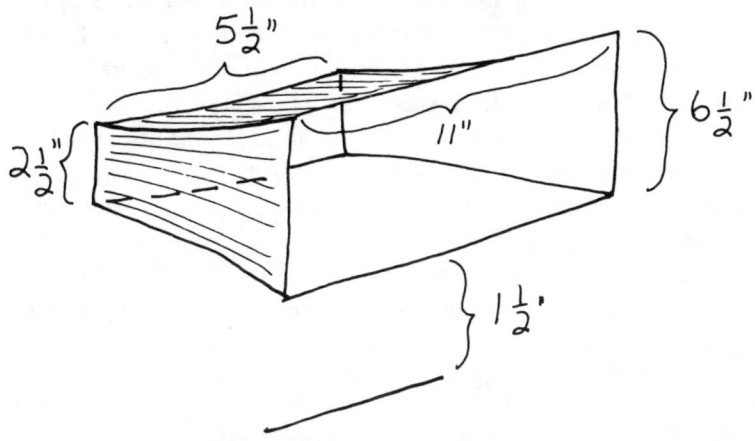

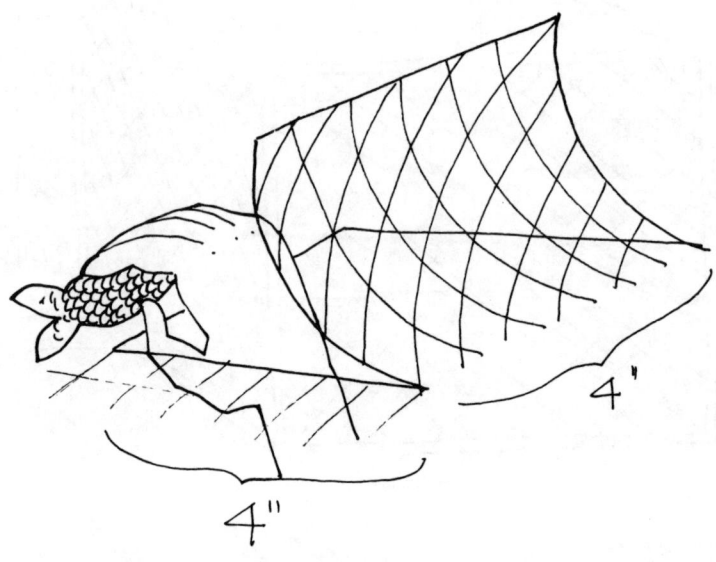

Bait is kept within a wire cylinder, five-and-a-quarter inches high, two-and-a-half inches in diameter, and covered on top. The crabs will enter the pot through the funnels to get at the bait, which can be tied to the wire, or even better, held in a cheesecloth bag, in turn fastened to the wire. After they are frustrated in attempts to reach the bait through the cylinder, the crabs will attempt to leave. This they will do in their normal fashion, by rising in the water. As they rise, they will meet a partition of chicken wire inside the pot. It is attached to the sides of the pot as shown. The first four-and-a-half inches on each side of the partition, as shown, are parallel to the floor of the pot which is six inches below. From there, the partition slopes upward at an angle of 45 degrees. Each side of the slope is fifteen-and-a-half inches. The two sides do not meet at an angle but instead curve towards one another, allowing for a roof, as shown, an inch wide. In this roof, cut an opening eight inches long and three inches wide. The crabs will rise through this opening into the top part of the pot, which serves as a holding chamber. You can remove the crabs by undoing the wire at the side of the pot, giving access to the holding chamber.

Crabbing with a Net

Scooping up crabs with a long-handled net is a traditional, time-tested way to catch them for the individual table. The net should have a long handle, about five feet is a good length, with mesh openings no more than an inch wide, like the type used in trotlining. Blue crabs, especially, like to rest in the shallow water an inch or two deep next to the edge of tidal creeks. If you quietly walk along the top of the bank, peering down, you will spot them. The net must be lowered slowly into the water -- jerky movements frighten crabs -- and edged close to the crab, behind it if at all possible. Once the net is near the crab, and preferably slightly under it, scoop it up as fast as you can.

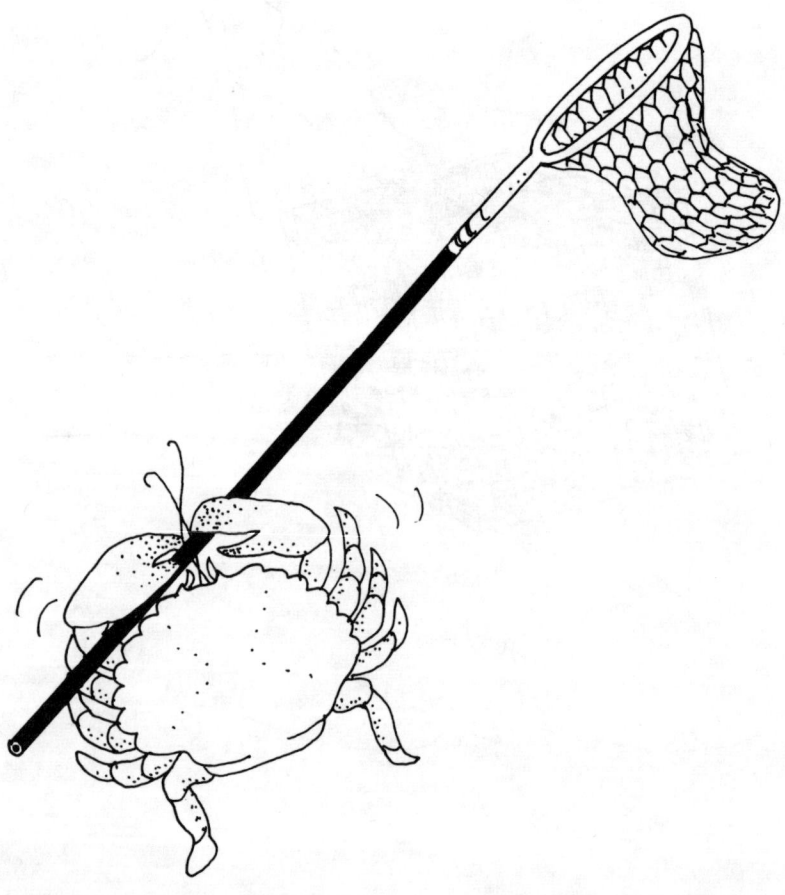

If you have a flat-bottomed boat, a canoe, or kayak, you can sneak up on the crabs from the water. While a friend gently paddles, lie along the bow of the craft and net the crabs from this position. The technique for netting by boat is the same as from land.

Handlining crabs from shore or a boat is fun and very productive when used in conjunction with a net. Tie a chicken neck or piece of fish to a cord. Drop or toss it into the water. If there are crabs on the bottom, they will quickly find the bait. Usually they reveal their presence by tugging on the line, or even moving it. Once you feel a crab, draw in the line very slowly. Do not make sudden movements or jerk the cord. The crab will follow the bait, ripping at it with its claws. It may even

try to pull the bait away. If the crab lets go -- when this happens the line goes slack -- leave the bait where it is. Chances are in a moment or two the crab will return. Continue drawing in the cord until the crab is within range of the net. While the crab is occupied with the bait, snatch it up in the net. I find that handlining and netting from a boat are excellent ways to catch crabs in tidal marshes.

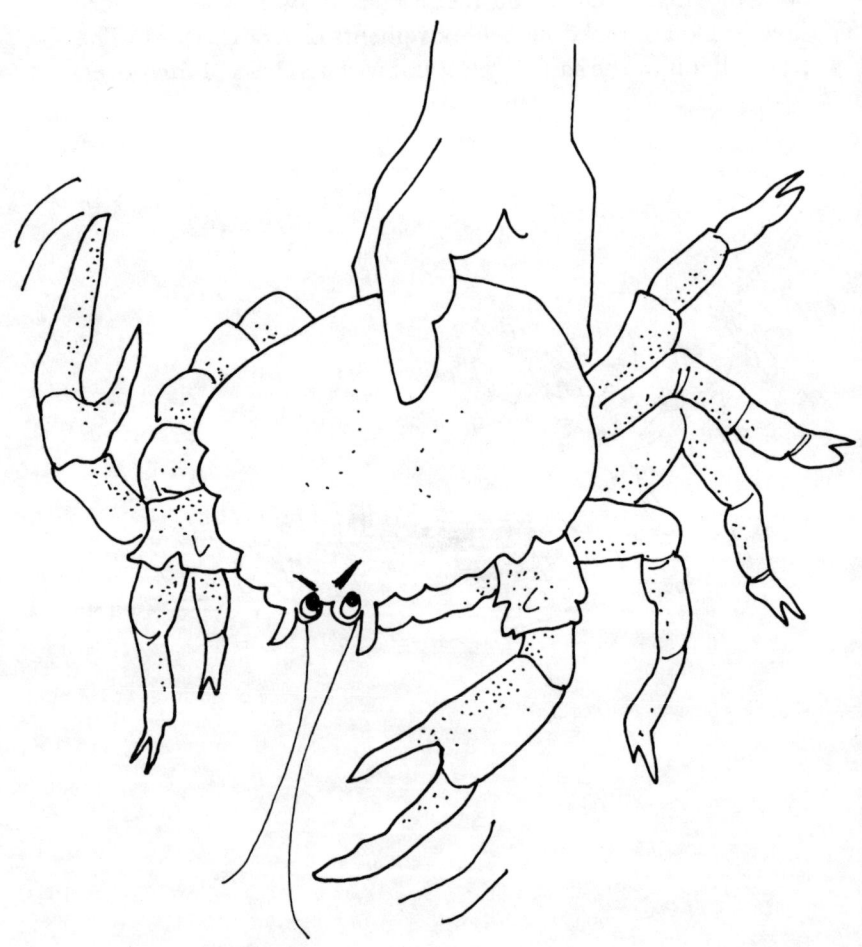

Once You've Caught 'Em, What to Do

Handling crabs, especially the kind with big pincers, requires caution. Don't put your fingers in the way of the pincers. Rather, hold the crab by the rear of the shell, between your thumb and fingers. It doesn't matter whether your thumb is atop or below the crab. This grip keeps the pincers far from your flesh. Metal tongs also may be used, and are a good idea if you are picking up crabs from a container that holds several of them. Crabs in a net sometimes cling to the mesh with their claws. Don't fight them. Try to shake them out of the net on to the ground, or bottom of the boat. If they continue to hold on, invert the netting and put the crab down. Sensing it is free to go, the crab will release its grip. Then you can grab it.

As noted, laws covering crabs vary according to states, even countries, so before you keep a crab, make sure you know if it is of legal size and sex. Some species, however, may not be covered by law in your area.

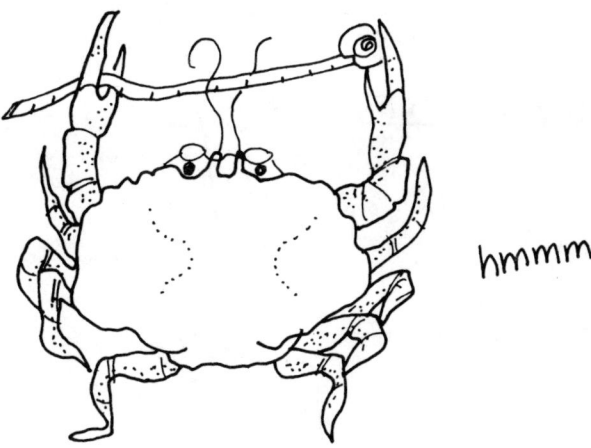

Storing Crabs

Newly-caught crabs can be kept in a covered plastic bucket or bushel, or in a wet burlap sack. Dampness is important in keeping crabs alive out of the water. So is keeping them out of the direct sun. If you can refrigerate them, all the better. Their life out of water is increased by chilling. However you store them, though, get them to the pot as soon as you can. The fresher they are the better they taste. Warning: keep the storage container tightly covered or your meal will climb out and slip away.

Cooking Crabs

As a safeguard to your health, one precaution is extremely important. It relates not to where you catch the crabs, but to how you store them once you have cooked them. Cooking by steaming or boiling destroys any harmful bacteria that might be on the crabs. Never let cooked crabs come into contact with live crabs, or any table surface, basket, or bucket that has held uncooked crabs. If this occurs, bacteria from the uncooked crabs may contaminate and spoil the cooked ones.

There is one tried-and-true classic recipe for cooking crabs, especially blue crabs. It is a method developed in the heart of crab country, Maryland's Chesapeake Bay area. The recipe is for a dozen crabs. Alter ingredient amounts if you use more or fewer crabs. You will need a big pot, large enough to hold all your crabs. The best kind is a real steamer, with a false, perforated bottom. Some steamers have a small pot with a perforated bottom nestled within a larger one.

Maryland Steamed Crab

Put two inches of liquid in the bottom of a steamer. The liquid should be of vinegar and water, a cup each is about right. Bring the liquid to a boil. Place the crabs in the pot in layers. Sprinkle each layer with a mixture made of three tablespoons of salt and two-and-a-half tablespoons of sea-food seasoning (some stores stock seasoning specially made for crabs). Steam for a least a half hour.

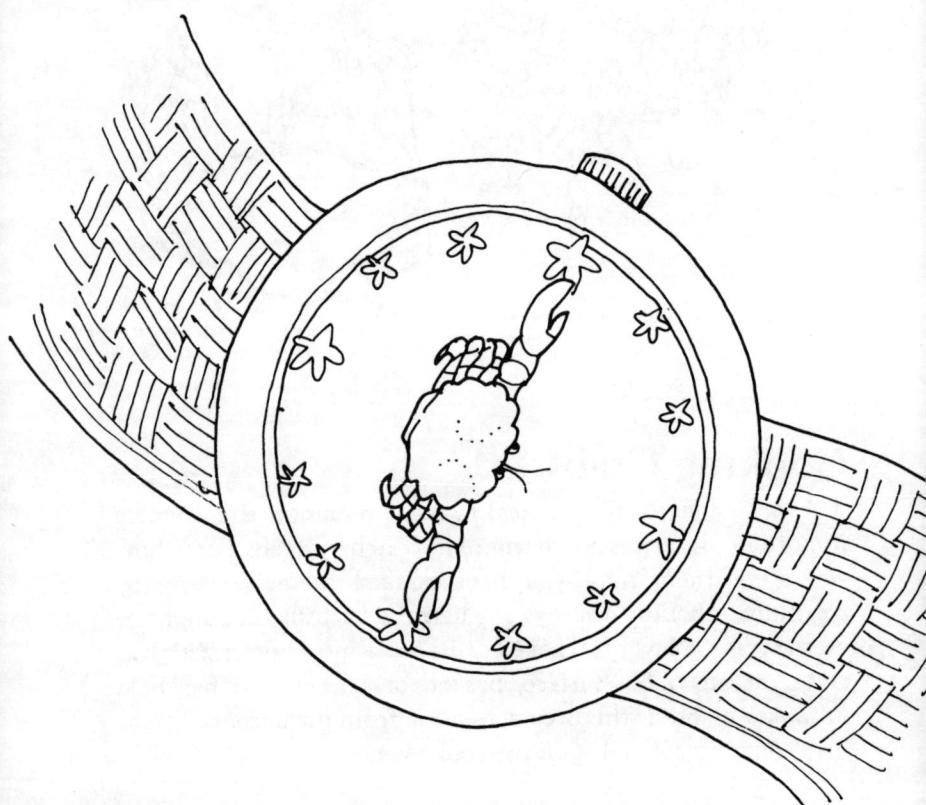

The Art of Eating Crabs

When your crabs are cooked, you are ready for a real feast. If you want to do it a traditional Maryland way, forget about dishes and a tablecloth. Cover the table with brown wrapping or bag paper. Put the crabs on the paper, and get ready to eat.

To glean all the meat from the crab, a special technique is necessary. First pull off the apron of the crab. Then peel off the top shell. Take a sharp knife, and cut away the legs inside the knuckle joints. Clean away the gills and internal organs, although you may want to save the liver (it's yellow), because it's tasty. Now the meat is exposed. Cut between it and the bottom shell, and lumps of succulent white meat are ready for eating. You

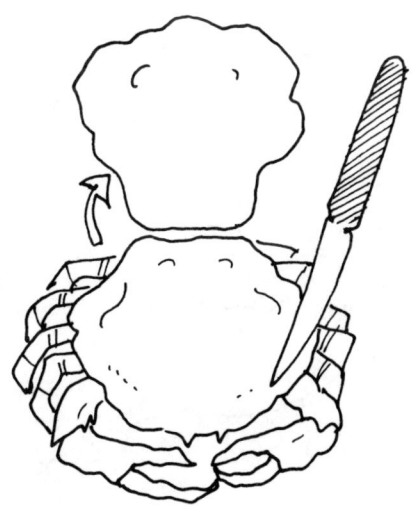

can use your knife to take the lumps out in whole pieces.

To get at the meat in the claws, you'll need a hammer, or if you have one, a wooden mallet. The latter is a traditional crab-cracking implement. Hold down the leg and claw with your knife as shown, and rap hard with the hammer. Pick away the remaining shell, and eat. Wash the meat down with cold beer or iced tea.

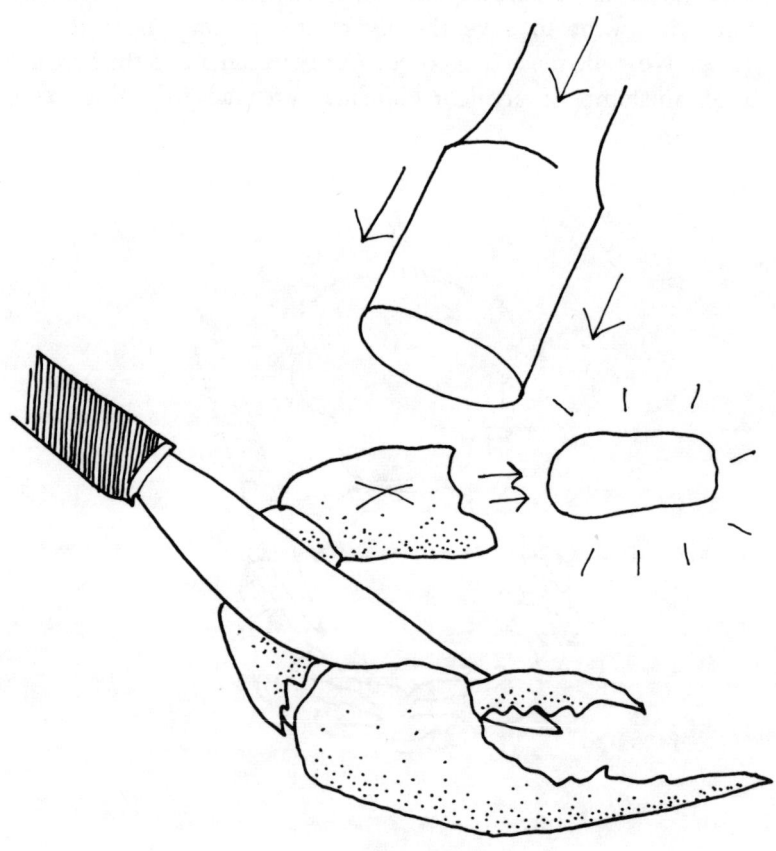

Softshell crabs, much less common than the hard-shell phase, are a true delicacy. The shells are thin enough to be eaten and are unusually tasty. Softshells are cleaned in the same way as the normal crab. They can be dipped in a batter of bread crumbs and butter, and fried in deep oil at 375° F for five minutes. When they are toasty brown, they are ready to eat -- with lemon and perhaps tartar sauce.

Softshells also can be prepared on an outdoor charcoal grill.

Barbecued Crab

For six people, use a dozen crabs.

3/4 cup of chopped parsley
1/2 cup melted fat or oil
1 tsp. lemon juice
1/4 tsp. nutmeg
1/4 tsp. soy sauce
dash liquid hot pepper sauce
lemon wedges

Place the crabs in a hinged, long-handled grill, well greased. Combine all the other ingredients except for the lemon. Keep the crabs about four inches over moderately hot coals for eight minutes, basting liberally. Turn and cook seven to ten minutes on the other side. When the crabs are lightly browned, serve with the lemon. Remember, you can eat virtually every part of the softshell.

3. CONCHS

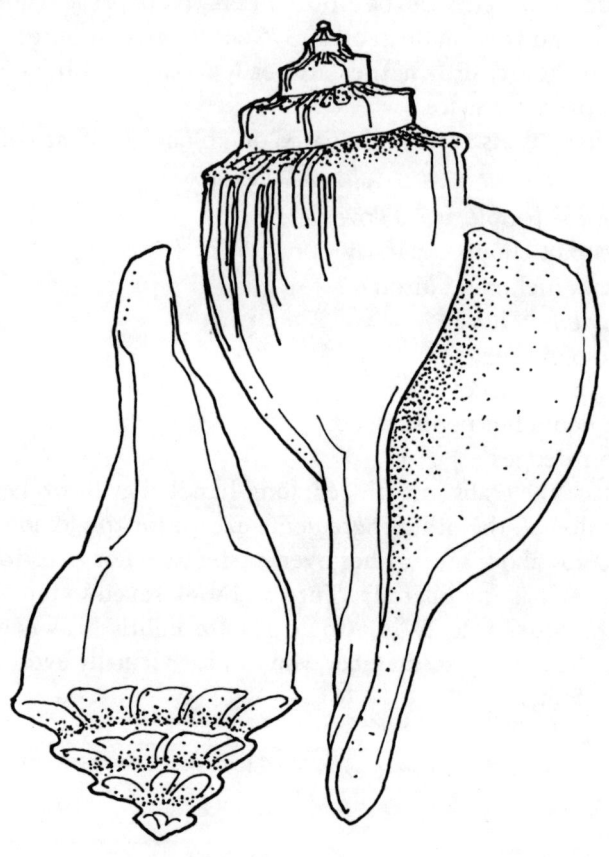

Conchs *(Busycon)*, also called winkles or whelks, inhabit the sea from the intertidal to depths of about sixty feet along most of the northeastern coast. The ones that are best for eating are the channeled species *(B. canaliculatum)* and the knobbed *(B. carica)*. They look very similar, with large, whorled shells often more than a half foot from top to bottom. No other marine snails in this area are so large. The chief difference is that channels line the shell of one species and knobs crown the other.

Conches have been eaten for ages by various peoples around the world, including West Indians, Bahamians, and Italians, who call conchs "scungili." There is a growing commercial fishery for conchs in the northeast. Most of the catch is sold to producers of shellfish chowders. Recipes for cooking conchs will be given later in the chapter.

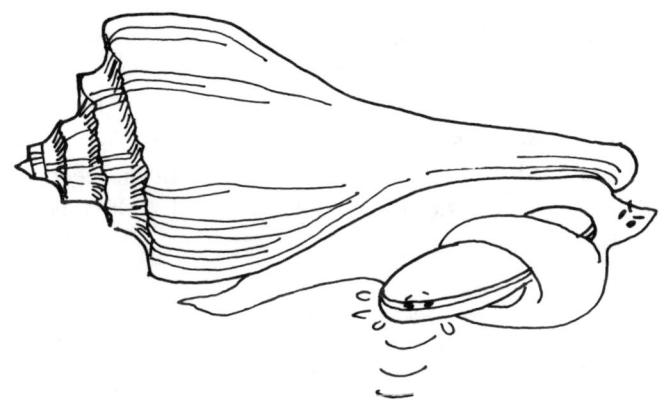

Conch Life Style

Conchs are predators and scavengers. They eat virtually any flesh they can find on the sea bottom. Their natural prey, however, consists of oysters, clams, and similar shellfish. Typically, the conch holds the prey in its muscular foot -- which is what you eat -- and breaks open the shell of the victim with blows of its own shell. Then the conch inserts its tongue, covered with raspy projections, and eats the helpless shellfish.

Conchs are incredibly abundant and not at all crafty. You can catch them in a lobster pot, or in a special trap that really is a simplified version of the lobster pot, but open at the top, without funnels, and lacking special "rooms."

Making a Conch Pot

To make a conch pot, you will need the following materials.
-- framing, ten pieces one-and-a-quarter by one by eighteen inches
-- twenty-four laths, one-and-a-half by a quarter by twelve inches
-- a lath two by a half by eighteen inches
-- eight laths, one-and-a-half by a quarter by eighteen inches
-- two bricks
-- twine
-- galvanized nails, 3d and 8d sizes
-- also four nails approximately three inches long, of any kind with a large, flat head.

Use the 8d nails to assemble the frame, which is a square. The 3d nails are used to attach the laths. The eight eighteen-inch laths are used on the floor of the pot. Notice that the top is left

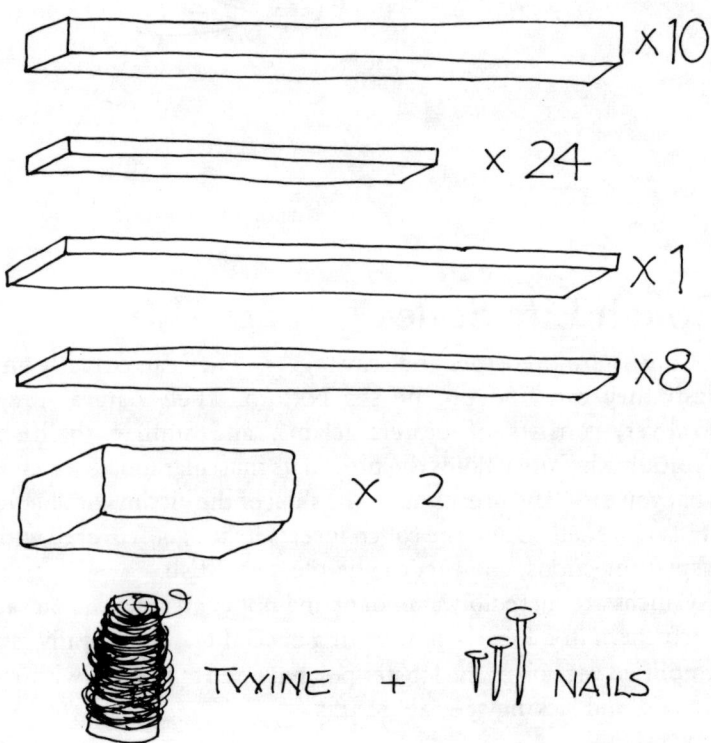

open. The twelve-inch laths are used for the four sides. Nail them vertically, as shown. The remaining lath is nailed across the open top of the pot.

The vertical position of the side laths enables the conch to creep up the outside of the trap without breaking the suction of its foot, as would be the case if the laths were horizontal, as on a lobster pot. Once the conch reaches the top of the pot, it falls inside the pot. You may wonder why the conch does not climb right out again. It would, except that twine is stretched around the circumference of the pot inside the top frame. The three-inch nails hold the twine, which the conch is unable to cross. The bricks are tied to the bottom of the pot as weight.

Pot Fishing for Conchs

Rigging a line and buoy for a conch pot is the same as for a lobster pot. The line need not be very long, as you seldom have to go deeper than about fifteen feet to catch conchs. Use your charts and find places to set your pots where the bottom is sandy or muddy, as this is the best habitat for conchs. For bait, you can use any of the lobster baits. Better yet, try the favorite bait of commerical conch fishermen in New England — the body of the horseshoe crab. The bait can be placed in the conch pot just as in a lobster pot, or simply tied to the bottom with twine. Conchs may be caught at almost any time of year, but from the middle Atlantic states north, autumn is the best season.

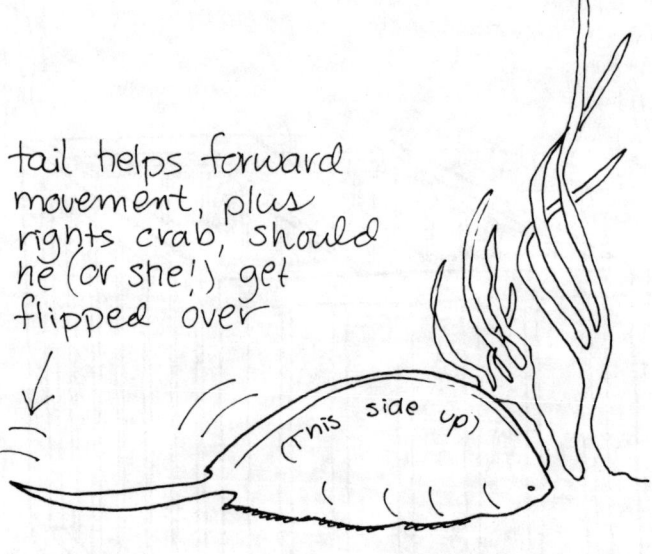

Horseshoe crab

Preparing Conchs

The first step in preparing conchs is to remove them from the shell. This can be done by steaming them for several minutes, until they can be easily removed with your fingers. The part of the conch that you eat is its large, fleshy foot. Attached to this is soft, gooey material, the innards and the rest of the body. Cut this away. Next, after washing the conchs, place them in a pot of water and boil for a half hour. Remove the conchs and let them drain for a few minutes.

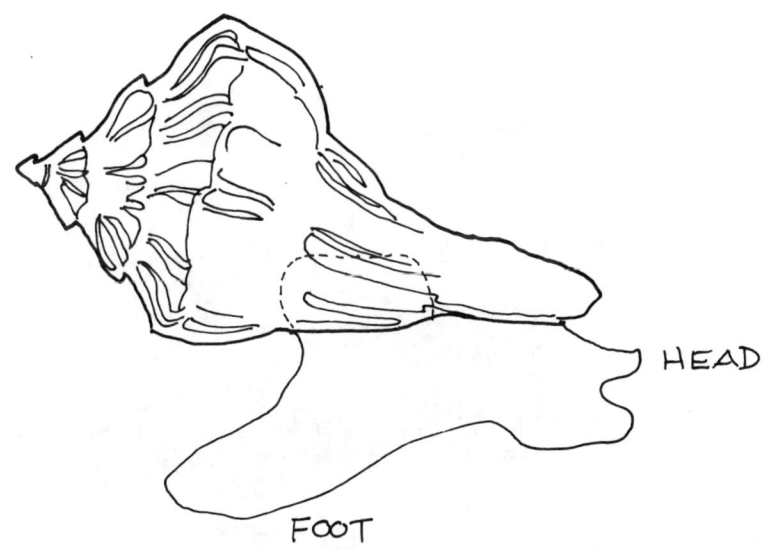

The meat can be finely chopped and added to tomato sauce for a nice topping on pasta. Even better, in my mind, is conch salad. To make, it, slice the meat thinly -- the thinner the better. Place the slices in a bowl. Cover with oil -- preferably olive oil. Add a touch of vinegar, to taste, and do the same with lemon juice. Salt and pepper the mix. A little paprika and a dash of liquid hot pepper sauce creates more zip, if that is to your liking. As a final ingredient, add slices of onion. Let the mix stand, covered in the refrigerator, overnight.

Serve the conch on a bed of lettuce. Depending on taste, you can season it even further with lemon, hot sauce, or vinegar. It makes either a main or side dish. Italian bread is nice with the salad.

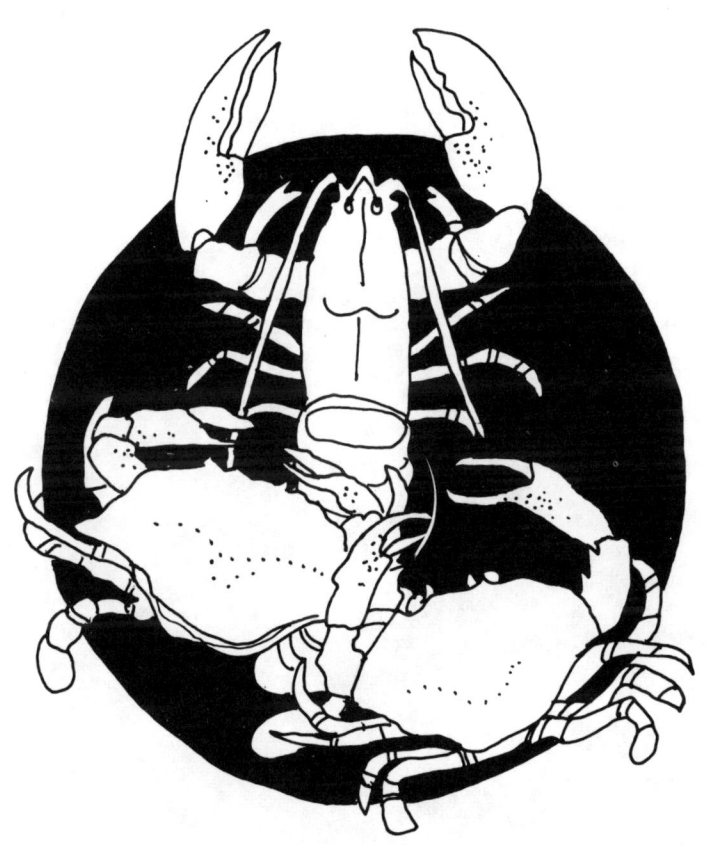

Notes

Record the date, time of day, and how long pots set, bait, weather, location, depth, distance from shore and *catch*.
GOOD RECORDS MAKE FOR GOOD CATCHES.

Notes

Notes

Notes

Notes